The Forager's Ho

[5 in 1]

The Most Complete Guide to Locating, Identifying, Harvesting, and Preparing Edible Wild Plants | 100+ Quick & Easy Recipes Included!

Table of Contents

Introduction

A warm day in the summer is the ideal time to go outdoors and take pleasure in the natural world, including foraging, which is a vital component of the whole experience. Because of this, even those who do not have an interest in eating wild plants will be fascinated to learn more about the plant that their friend boldly chose and consumed, since everyone likes a delightful surprise. It makes no difference how far we have strayed from the natural world; we all retain a lingering passion for hunting and gathering since it was the only way ancient people could ensure their own survival.

When we eat food that comes from the wild, it serves as a reminder that our bodies are sustained by the elements of nature, such as the sun, the rain, and the soil, rather than by the products sold in those vast stores. Even if great progress has been made in contemporary technology, taking even a minor quantity of nourishment from the globe results in an environmental imbalance that acts as a constant reminder of our need on the natural world. As a direct consequence of this, we are unable to create even the most basic requirements for our survival.

In the twenty-first century, activities such as hunting and gathering could be seen as archaic by certain people. Foraging is just as important as it has ever been for those of us who want to live lives that are healthy, happy, and fulfilling and who want to be able to pass on these benefits to the generations who come after us.

What are Edible Wild Plants?

Edible wild plants are wild foods derived naturally. They are available in various forms, including vegetables, fresh edible plants, fresh mushrooms, and fresh fruits. They originate from flowers and comprise several parts, each having a unique identity and function. In a wasteland, wild vegetables and plants grow. Wild mushrooms also grow in the wasteland, but only during the rainy season.

Humans have depended on wild edible plants for centuries, and many of the domesticated plants consumed today were once wild edible plants. Wild plants are an integral part of human food systems and diet, and while humans have made progress in food production over the years, wild edible plants still play a role in boosting food availability.

Benefits of Consuming Wild Edible Plants

Wild edible plants are not domesticated or cultivated, meaning they grow naturally. If properly harnessed, these plants contribute immensely to poverty eradication, malnutrition alleviation, income generation, agricultural diversification, and food security.

Additionally, wild edible plants can empower local market actors and shorten the distance between the producers and consumers to diminish the unprecedented reliance on globalized value chains (Boutenko S., 2022). Many still experience hunger despite the improvement in the globalized food chain.

Wild edible plants can fill the gap successfully. The wild plants can, therefore, help to prevent or correct malnutrition. They provide greater dietary diversity and have endless health-giving properties. Additionally, they can treat several ailments as herbal medicine in phytotherapy (Clay R, 2001).

Studies show that wild edible plants are rich in fiber, microelements, antioxidants, flavonoids, phenols, and vitamins. What is more, their nutritional components are more than what is present in cultivated plants. Cultivated plants may be contaminated by chemicals, including pesticides, which are not present in wild edible plants. Wild plants can also be rich in several dietary supplements, bioactive compounds, flavors, and colors unavailable in cultivated plants.

Since there is a relationship between disease and dietary factors, consuming pure, healthy, wild edible plants can prevent many diseases. The wild edible plants also meet the criteria of a healthy diet. They are even recognized as Intangible Cultural Heritage of Humanity, becoming a global symbol of healthy lifestyle and food. It can protect the body against chronic disease development, including cancer and diabetes. Additionally, they have environmental and socio-economic sustainability, meaning consuming them can provide cultural ecosystem services.

More experts pay attention to wild edible plants, attempting to process and preserve them without damaging their natural compositions. Its reliability as a source of healthy natural products can foster biochemical research towards documenting their main bioactive products and various nutritional properties. Studies are also underway to investigate how wild edible plants can combine with other ingredients to improve their nutritional and sensory qualities. Some experts are also working on finding innovative cooking methods to prevent damage to their natural nutrients. Many cultivated foods get their nutrients damaged during the food preparation process.

Why You Should Forage

Foraging refers to the act of seeking for and acquiring food supplies or therapeutic plants in the forest. Foragers may be looking for either edible or medicinal plants. When stepping out into the natural environment, travelers who are going to be there for an extended period, such as on a camping trip or an excursion into the wilderness, may need to rely on foraging for additional food or for their own survival. In this situation, being able to recognize plants that can be eaten is a talent that might save your life.

Many wild plants that are often disregarded, not because they are of no benefit to the body but because the widespread perception is that these plants are detrimental to the body. However, foraging allows you to discern between dangerous and edible species.

Before you go out into the wilderness to scavenge for food, you should have some awareness on the very few harmful species that live there and when searching for edible plants, it will make you feel better if you have some idea of what kinds of plants you could come across that are toxic.

Cattails, acorns, stinging nettles, tubers, rosehips, weeds, plantains, and yarrow are some of the frequent food items that may be found via foraging. Foraging is something you should not do until you know how to do it safely, because eating some plants can be bad for your health. Here are some of the reasons why you should forage.

It is Affordable and Accessible

Local libraries may assist you in locating edible plants in your yard. Botanists and mycologists can identify photographs submitted by foragers online. Excursions are organized by local groups to educate people about wild foods and proper gathering, so you are close to edible food no matter where you live. With technology and community, foraging may become more affordable and accessible.

It is Environmentally Friendly

Foraging is the most ecologically beneficial method to eat, as wild plants and mushrooms do not need to be watered. There are methods to forage ethically, unlike some store plant-based meals. Mushroom foraging resembles fruit plucking. Both the tree and the mycelium produce fruits to pass on seeds and spores. Foraging helps mushroom cultivation and spore spread. Gathering parasitic mushrooms may aid nearby trees. In "bump years" like 2020, there is more food than local wildlife can eat. Gleaning from nature's garden is the most eco-friendly alternative.

It Fosters Connection with Community

We have a fun time and learn a lot about the local ecosystem when on hunts with your friends and relatives. This kind of entertainment draws one closer to the area and makes things like walking in the woods a community-building opportunity.

It is Fun

Many people relax by hunting and fishing in nature. It is not essential to give up hunting if you embrace a plant-based diet, and vice versa. Every walk in the woods is a treasure hunt since you never know what you may discover in the event. Over two hundred edible mushrooms and hundreds of edible shoots, leaves, seeds, flowers, and roots exist and its fulfilling to find these plants within their niche.

It is Easier Than Growing Food

Food production requires endless time, money, and care. To produce healthy food in your garden, you must either buy soil or add compost and take efforts to protect your crops from wild predators. Finally, you must know when, where, how, and when to care for seeds as they grow.

Book 1: Categories of Edible Wild Plants

Herbs, Trees, and Shrubs

Examples of edible wild trees and shrubs are:

- Adam's needle

- Autumn olive

- Black chokeberry

- Black raspberry

- Common barberry

- Common blueberry

- Common chokeberry

- Common hawthorn

- Common juniper

- Eastern redbud

- Eastern white cedar

- Eastern white pine

- Elderberry

- Ginkgo

The plants are available in different regions, tropical and temperate. Their branches also vary in size, same with their heights. Even the leaves are edible and applicable to natural medicines. Some people also claim to use flowers as herbs. Most of them equally produce edible fruits.

Buckwheat Family

Wild buckwheat features an annual root system and has ocrea at each node. Their flowers are generally small. It is a yearly summer vine common in the annual cropping systems. The buckwheat family of wild edible plants has heart-shaped leaves. They have stems if 60 inches. Their flowers lack petals, while their sepals are white to greenish and five in number. They grow between June and August.

Their leaves can reach a maximum of 2.5 inches, but some have leaves reaching only a length of one inch. When they mature, they can form an extensive shade, spreading over other plants nearby.

Garlic Mustard

Garlic mustard is a biennial herb labeled as an invasive weed by many people. The plant originated from Europe and is highly nutritious. It now has a broad representation in North America, and its blooming period lies between May and June, during which harvesters can access it. The plant has several benefits, including cancer prevention, lowering cholesterol, heart protection, and weight loss.

Its leaves can be either kidney-shaped or heart-shaped, while its flowers are petite and easy to recognize. The sepals are only four and are usually green. Unlike the Buckwheat family, the garlic mustard flower has petals, but the number of petals is four.

Nettle Family

There are different categories of plants belonging to the Nettle Family, but only the Stinging Nettle and Wood Nettle are edible. They are also highly nutritious. You can quickly locate them in the woodlands and even in your backyard. The wood nettle originated from Central North and Eastern America, while the stinging nettle was only introduced to this location.

The plants pass through different stages of development and are edible at each stage. They are tender and nice-looking when young. But the coarseness becomes more visible as they grow older. You should avoid harvesting nettle plants near the road or the ones you are unsure about.

Knotweed

Knotweed is yet another edible wild plant, but it has a distinctive taste from others. The plant tastes like lemony rhubarb, which you can add to a series of dishes. It originates from Japan and is rich in several nutrients, including Vitamin A and Vitamin C. Studies show that consuming the plant can treat and prevent cognitive disorders.

The plant is good to eat. It arrived in Europe in the 19th century, bought in by a migrating botanist, forming the foundation for its broad reach in the country. Its growth rate is incredible, making it a readily available food source.

Chickweed

Chickweed is an edible wild plant. Nevertheless, you must consume it with care since an excess consumption can cause stomach upset consequent from the saponoids present in the plant. You can even eat the leaves and flowers raw if you so desire or cook them if it is convenient. The plant's fresh leaves and flowers can be included in your salad, along with pesto, stews, or stir-fries.

Chickweed is highly nutritious, and even its seed is useful as you can grind it into a powder to make thick soup or bread. It flourishes easily but disappears during the winter months.

Purslane

Purslane originated from Persia and India. It has, however, spread across the globe, becoming one of the favorite foods for those interested in edible wild plants. Its leaves are succulent and fleshy, with its yellow flowers adding a unique glow to them. The plants resemble baby jade too.

There is a close relationship between the plant and Rose Moss. The plant can last for up to 40 years from germination before dying off completely, making it a long-term food source. It can, however, take up to three weeks before developing flowers following seed germination.

Book 2: How to Locate Edible Wild Plants

Begin with edible plants that are easy to identify and easy to find. Consider searching for chanterelle mushrooms if you have a fungus-related interest. When the time and place are right, they are easy to find, and it is simple to differentiate them from non-edible plants that have a strong resemblance.

Study of the plant's environment. Backyards, on the other hand, are excellent areas to look for wild food plants. Cattails and ramps are two examples of plants that are not likely to be found in swamps or on steep slopes, respectively, so targeting specific areas may help narrow your search for these wild plants

Keep track of wild edible plants throughout the year so that you can identify perennial species that you may harvest at the start of the growing season. By the time pokeweed is identified, it is often too late to use it. However, if you take note of its position while it is still visible throughout the summer, may as well win you a weed after its appearance in first spring.

Discover more about the plants that go well together. They may as well make it easier for you to discover the location. Many varieties of plants are often seen growing near other types of plants. For instance, if you come across yellow dock, there is a strong possibility that you will also come across pokeweed in the area.

Buckwheat Family

The plant grows naturally on waste areas, roadsides, and fields. You can also find it on irregularly mowed lawns. It is a fast-growing plant and thrives very well in the northern temperate regions, like the north part of the United States. In abundance, you can also find it in the southwestern part of Asia, including Russia. The shrub is native to northwestern Mexico and the southwestern United States.

The plant prefers well-drained, light to medium soils for growth, like silt soil, loans, and sandy loams. It cannot thrive satisfactorily on soil containing a lot of limestones, wet soils, or heavy soils. It prefers moist, cool conditions and cannot tolerate frost or drought.

Garlic Mustard

Garlic mustard can grow best in a plain forest, upland, savanna, and roadside. You can find the plant in disturbed areas or trail edges too. It grows well in open areas but can also tolerate shades. It is better to check the shaded floors of moist deciduous forests where it grows best when looking for it. Residents of the United States can find it all through the Midwestern and northeastern states, spreading from South Carolina to Canada, including North Dakota and Kansas. If you reside in Europe, you can find garlic mustard growing naturally in southern Italy, Germany, Sweden, and Czechoslovakia, including eastern England.

Nettle Family

You can find members of the nettle family growing in various places, like woodlands, fields, hedgerows, and gardens. The plants also thrive tremendously in fertile, damp, disturbed ground, making them good colonizers of places where human activities occur, like development and agriculture.

The yield obtainable depends on the soil quality and available moisture. You can find it on the edges of meadows, streams, and pastures. The plant loves the moist area, but the land must not be waterlogged. The area may be shaded or even under the sun; the plant can still grow well there. Studies show that nettles require about four hours of sunlight per day in the summer.

Knotweed

Knotweed is a highly tolerant plant. Consequently, it can grow in a variety of places. The plant can thrive in drought, heat, salinity, and even deep shade. You can equally find it close to water sources, like rivers and streams. It grows in old home sites, utility rights-of-way, waste places, ditches, and other low-lying areas. In summary, you can find this plant virtually anywhere. The plant is ready for harvesting in early spring, especially in the first two weeks of May. However, it usually starts flowering by the end of May to early August.

Chickweed

You can find chickweed in a shaded, moist, and cool area. It also grows well as a weed on cultivated gardens, pastures, and fields. Many have reported finding it under trees and shrubs. The edible wild plant also grows well on roadsides. The plant is an annual winter weed commonly found in Florida landscapes. Some other names it bears are winter weed, common chickweed, and chickenwort.

The plant prefers soil rich in nitrogen and has neutral pH. However, it also grows on soils with different pH.

Purslane

Purslane is a weed, and you can find it growing in gardens. Therefore, the plant is not picky and can grow in varieties of soil conditions. However, you can find it mostly on drier soils. The plant prefers a sunny area since its seeds require adequate sunlight to germinate. Remember that purslane is an annual plant, and you can harvest its seeds once a year.

Book 3: Easy Identification of Edible Wild Plants

Many of the wild plants we have around are good for eating, but we still need to be careful when choosing wild plants since not all of them are edible. If care is not taken, one may end up consuming poison. The edible ones are full of nutrients that can positively impact our lives. Mark you, the edible ones may not be tasty, but that does not mean they do not contain helpful nutrients that can positively impact our lives. So, how can you be sure that the wild plant you are looking at is edible or not? We will provide helpful answers to the question in the remaining part of this write-up.

Finding the Right One to Eat

Some of the poisonous wild plants can look like the edible ones. If care is not taken, you would have consumed poison before realizing that you did. Studies show that many wild plants around are similar in appearance to the Italian parsley. A good example of such plants is hemlock, once used as a poison to kill Socrates, the great Greek philosopher. So, never eat that wild plant, except you can recognize precisely what it is.

One of the best ways to know if that plant is right to eat is by smelling it. Wild onions are edible wild plants. You can pick out the right one to eat among them by smelling them. If a non-almond smells like almond, you should steer clear of it because it is likely a poisonous wild plant.

Nibble the Tree's Nut

One of the best ways to know if that plant is poison is by nibbling on its nut. The fattier more calorie-dense plants are good edible wild plants. Tree nuts are excellent choices in this regard, and you can find them in abundance in many of the North American woodlands. Hickory nuts are in abundance in the eastern part of the Great Plains, and they are examples of edible wild plants. They are also rich in protein and hard to crack into. You can quickly identify them by their outer husk and inner shell, enveloping a nut meat that looks like a brain. They will taste like pecans too. They can equally be consumed without cooking. The nuts will look veiny, just like pecan.

Then, which plants specifically should you be keeping an eye out for? Those plant components that are fattier and more calorie-dense should be your first choice if you want to remain healthy.

Go looking for hickory nuts if you are east of the Great Plains. Hickory nuts are one of the wild plant foods that have the highest calorie density. These high-protein treats are difficult to break into since the trees that produce them are towering seasonal hardwoods. They feature an outer husk and an interior shell that surrounds the nut flesh. But if you do, it will be well worth your time and effort. They taste like pecans, which originate from a southern hickory species, and you do not need to cook or soak them. Be certain that the nut has a veiny appearance, much like a pecan. Buckeye nuts, which may be deadly, have two shells like hickory nuts do, but the flesh inside of buckeye nuts has a radically distinct appearance; it is smooth and spherical.

The protein-rich hickory nut is a tasty treat but be careful not to consume it in the same manner as the deadly buckeye.

Pine nuts from the Pinyon pine, a scrubby evergreen of the high desert, are another fantastic alternative to consider if you find yourself lost in the woods of the American southwest. These nuts are simple to harvest and have a flavor like that of buttery kernels; they are prepared to inspire any pesto. Pine nuts that you buy at the grocery store are often imports, yet native Americans and chefs have been using pinyon pine nuts in their cuisine for years.

Even the lowly acorn may be eaten if prepared properly. Native Americans relied heavily on these animals as a source of primary nutrition. However, they need to make sure they are well prepared. To begin with, remove the nuts from the shells with a rock. Using a clean sock, soak the nut flesh in a stream for days if you do not have a pot. Both its astringent flavor and the tannic acid, which, in high quantities, may cause stomach troubles.

Do the Berries Look Familiar?

If that berry looks familiar to the normal ones you see at grocery stores, it is probably not poisonous. You can confirm this by biting into it. Unfortunately, researchers have not developed any rule of thumb for identifying a poisonous berry. Only eat the berry if you can identify it. If you can find wild raspberries, blackberries, and some other popular berries, you can go for those with the assurance that they are not poisonous. You can stumble upon many of these popular wild berries in the northwestern part of the pacific. The Himalayan blackberries are especially common in these areas.

Almonds and berries may be combined to form a tasty dessert, which is also a reliable source of calories. However, choosing fruit that is safe to eat may be a struggle, since certain fruits may selectively cause illness. There is no solid rule of thumb for distinguishing between what is useful and what is detrimental. Limit yourself to the kind of berries whose identification of which you are certain. Look out for blackberries, raspberries, and other so-called "aggregate berries," for instance. These berries are known for their thick clusters of fruit. The widespread popularity of blackberries in the United States is owing to its great nutritional content and abundance in places.

Fruit clusters of aggregation berries, such as blackberries, raspberries, and other similar fruits, are easily identifiable from their distinctive cluster formation. Other well-known fruits may be found in a variety of locations. Elderberries, for example, are small, purplish-black berries that form a cluster in the shape of an umbrella. Additionally, be vigilant of fruits that mimic blueberries or cherries in appearance; these berries and cherries may have a delicious taste, but they may have dangerous equivalents

Uproot the Plants

All aquatic plants with their leaves poking out of the water in lakes, wetlands, and rivers are edible wild plants. They are generally called emergent aquatics. These plants feature cigar-shaped flower spikes with their roots rich in carbs and proteins. They are better consumed cooked since they are fibrous. Eating them raw will not appeal to the appetite.

Look for plants with leaves that extend above the water's surface near a lake, river, or marsh. These emergent aquatic plants have delicious and nutritious roots that may be eaten whole.

Cattail, or bulrush, is a good backup. The cigar-shaped "flower spikes" of these plants are easy to spot. The fibrous roots are a reliable source of protein and carbs, despite being unpalatable when eaten raw. These water plants have edible roots and kindling-worthy cigar-shaped flower spikes.

Large arrowhead-shaped leaves identify this plant, also called "Katniss." Katniss is The Hunger Games' protagonist. Its underground tubers taste like sweet potatoes and are easy to dig out. Stomping in the mud loosens it, allowing the tubes to float.

Universal Edibility Test

Universal edibility testing may be used if the plant in question looks to be edible, but you are not sure whether it is safe. It involves consuming little amounts of a plant and gradually increasing the amount of time spent in physical contact with it to see whether any negative effects occur.

The below experiment must be conducted individually for every part of the plant that you wish to eat, such as the roots, the leaves, and the stem.

Take a good deep whiff of it. You should discard the plant part if it has a putrid odor. If this does not work, try pressing a part of the plant on the inside side of your elbow or wrist for a few minutes. Is there any itchiness, burning, or other undesirable reaction? In such a case, you should not consume it. If your skin does not seem to be reacting negatively, put the plant on your lips and then wait fifteen minutes.

Unless it is burning or itching, take a pea-sized bite. Spit out the plant quickly if it has a taste that is excessively bitter or soapy, but keep in mind that most plants taste horrible, so you should not expect much of the peppery tang of mint. Even if the flavor is tolerable, you should continue to keep the piece of food in your mouth for the next 15 minutes.

You need to hold off for at least a few hours. That section of the plant, and just that part, is safe to consume at this stage, assuming you are not ill or dead on the ground.

You may need to go through a botany book to correctly identify plants like wild mustard. These suggestions could make the prospect of being lost in the woods seem less terrifying, but they only scratch the surface of what engages in wild food gathering.

How can you know whether you are looking at compound or simple leaf? References might save you the trouble of recognizing the sort of plants in your area. However, to summarize the essential aspects to look for, the buds on the twigs and the twigs are both wooden in nature, while the midribs of compound leaves are not.

- Sniff the plant strongly. Throw it away if it smells like a rotting corpse or gives any awful smell.

- Hold it to your inner wrist or elbow for some minutes if it does not smell awful. It is not an edible plant if you feel any negative responses like burning or itching.

- If the plant doesn't cause any negative response, bring it close to your lips and kiss it. watch out for any reaction for about 15 minutes

- If you do not feel any negative sensation on your lips after 15 minutes, take a little bite from the plant. Spit it out immediately if it tastes soapy or bitter. However, if the taste is bearable, hold it in your mouth for an additional 15 minutes. When the 15 minutes expires, you can now swallow the plant.

- Wait for another one hour or any negative sensation in your stomach. If you do not feel anything negative after one hour, consider that part of the wild plant edible.

Know what not to eat

There are plenty that can be eaten, yet all it takes is one mistaken bite to be fatal. That is an exaggeration. But there are certain plants that you really need to stay away from at all costs. Be wary of edible-looking plants that are poisonous just because they have leafy petals. For instance, multiple species of wild parsley appear quite like hemlock, which is the plant that was used to make the poisonous drink that resulted in Socrates' demise. There is no need to know about harmful plants. To put it another way, you should never bite into anything until you are very certain in your identification of it.

Smell a plant to confirm it identify. For instance, you may find wild onions growing in woods all around the United States, and these onions are an excellent food source. If you have any doubts that the aroma does not match any recognizable cuisine, do not consume it. Additionally, you may use your sense of smell to identify toxic plants. You should avoid anything that is not an almond but smells like almonds since this might be an indication of the presence of cyanide, which is dangerous.

Book 4: Harvesting Edible Wild Plants Like a Pro

Wild edible plants need to be harvested with care lest you damage them. While they are wild and more resilient than the plants we cultivate, their nutrients may be affected, and their functions defeated if you do not harvest them carefully. Wrong harvesting can also kill the plant and prevent another stem from sprouting up from where you gathered the last one. This section will show you how to harvest wild edible plants to safeguard their nutrients and the environment.

Leaves may be regarded of as the most renewable plant resource. The phrase "cut-and-come again" refers to a strategy that is often used by gardeners, and it applies to many of the plants. This strategy entails going back to a plant many times throughout the course of the year to collect leaves that have recently grown. Pinch off a plant's developing tips above a node to stimulate leaf production from dormant lateral buds below.

Responsible foragers adhere to the guideline that they should never take all the leaves off a plant. This will either force the plant to lay seed suddenly and unexpectedly or put it under stress, which will allow for the germination of pests and diseases. This may harm a species' gene pool. A small number of tree species have leaves that are edible, and these species include several that produce substantial numbers of leaves.

Simple Harvesting Procedures

Take Only What You Need

When harvesting wild edible plants, you should only go for what you need and nothing more. If not, you may waste the plants and prevent others from accessing them. After harvesting, you can dry the plant to last for a long time. The dried plants can last for a long time, removing the need to harvest more than you need. They can even remain viable with their nutrients intact for about 12 months. You do not have to gather a lot of them with the hope of keeping them for many seasons; they will still be available next season. So, harvest enough to meet your needs for this season. When you come across a population of wild edible plants, only harvest about 5% of the population.

Harvest from Multiple Spots

You may not be the only one that has discovered the hidden benefits of consuming wild edible plants. So, many more people could have found your source and harvested from there. By the time you come for your harvest round, there may not be anything left for you. To ensure you always get your supply of wild edible plants, make sure you have multiple harvest spots. If wild edible pant harvesters have invaded one spot, go to your next spot instead of having a pointless argument.

Even if you are the only one having access to the spot, you should still look for multiple harvest spots so that you do not deplete the source. You can even rotate the spots each year.

Consider the following rules of thumb when harvesting edible wild plants:

- Harvest roots in fall only

- Harvest barks in spring before the tree starts flowering

- Harvest leaves in spring before they start flowering

- Harvest flowers in bloom only

- Harvest fruits only when they are ripe

- Harvest seeds only in the late fall.

Harvesting Stems

Ideally, cut stems using sharp secateurs, a pruning saw, or a knife immediately above a node. This releases dormant buds underneath the cut. It also protects the plant from a decaying dead stem infecting it.

Just before blossoming, cut the plant at ground level or carefully uproot it with a fork, shaking the roots. Biennial and herbaceous perennial growth should be limited. This helps the plant bloom.

Woody perennial plant portions should also be taken in insignificant amounts to allow the plant to regrow. Leave bigger branches a few millimeters above flush. Selective coppicing may be a good approach for multi-stemmed plants like hazel. This old harvesting method may revive plants and is versatile while Pre-flowering herbaceous stems are the hardest to harvest. With time and practice, you might get used to making harvest predictions based on what you know about a particular microclimate. Cow parsley (Anthriscus sylvestris) and alexanders (Smyrnium olusatrum) stems are some of the examples.

It is lovely when it is gentle, fragile, and youthful, and before eating you may need to remove the thin, fibrous outer skin. As plants grow, they become hard and fibrous, and within a few days, a plant portion might transform from delectable to inedible.

Harvesting Roots

According to most herbal treatment literature, autumn and spring are the best months to harvest roots. Busy people's time constraints will affect many of our decisions.

One of the favorite fall activities include gathering biennial and perennial roots. The plant will consume carbohydrates and other resources during this period before dormancy. During this time, the plant has more therapeutic components. When plants emerge from winter hibernation in the spring, they have drained their nutritional and water supplies.

Winter frosts transform complex carbohydrate reserves in spring-harvested roots into simple sugars. Therefore, spring-harvested roots taste better. Biennial roots are at their finest at the end of their first year. Digging and persuasion are needed to remove tap-rooted plants without injuring them. Draw a large circle around the plant's base, dig a hole along the circle's line, and pluck out the roots.

Harvesting Barks

When the sap starts rising in the spring, the bark is easy to peel off the tree. Evergreen and conifer tree bark may be harvested year-round.

Bark collection is easy. It is two-staged. Reduce and preparation. For medicinal barks like cramp bark, Berberis, and oak, three- to five-year-old branches are needed. Counting visible scars on wooden branches, called abscission points, may determine their age. They look like closely spaced waves on the stem. They grow where last year's buds burst.

Medicinal uses need the inner bark. This section contains plants' vascular systems, which pump sap. It consists of the continually dividing cambium cells and the xylem and phloem networks.

Phloem cells link a plant's leaves to the rest of the plant, whereas xylem cells connect its roots. The cambium layer of cells in every woody plant's stem, branch, and trunk constantly generates new cells, increasing the plant's diameter. All woody plants undergo this procedure.

Recent xylem cells are in the center of the trunk or branch on one side of the cambium. Phloem cells, on the other side of the cambium, are formed of spongy, corky tissue.

Because of this, you should remove the bark's softer phloem, cambium layer, and juvenile xylem cells. Spring harvest should readily peel inner barks.

Harvesting Leaf buds

This range of options of harvesting is by no means limitless. Sycamore blooms were preserved as food by being cooked in salt during the recent famines in Eastern Europe. After reading about how the inner bark of the lime tree may be ground into a flour component, harvest some lime tree buds that winter and try making a salt-boiled dish do not give up on your first trial as it will not be easy to get that taste that you desire.

After harvesting the wild edible plants, you should process them without delay to avoid losing their nutrients or decaying.

Safety Considerations While Harvesting Wild Edible Plants

You should never harvest your wild edible plants from a contaminated environment. You should avoid environments where toxic wastes are dumped since they can affect the plants, making them poisonous. Is there a drought in the area where the plant is growing? You do not want to harvest the wild edible plants in a drought as this can cause the already distressed plant to go into extinction, which you must avoid.

You should familiarize yourself with the right way to harvest the plants without killing them. You will be saving yourself from hunger next season and protecting the soil from erosion.

Never forget to wear protective gear when harvesting wild edible plants. The plants are growing in the wild, where you will have some other harmful plants. If some injurious plants touch your skin directly, they can lead to unwanted allergic reactions, like anaphylactic reaction, which is life-threatening. Aside from unfriendly plants, you may also encounter animals and flies that sting or bite you in the wild. The protective gears can protect you from any injury.

Book 5: Simple Preparation Processes for Edible Wild Foods

Edible wild food preparation involves proper storage and handling. We will elaborate on how to store than right in this chapter.

Proper Storage

The wild edible plants can be prepared fresh, or you can store them for later use. The best way to keep them is first to dry them, and you can use a dehydrator for that. If you do not have a dehydrator, you can hang them in small bunches to dry in the sun or over low heat in the oven.

- You can either slice the mushroom uniformly or leave it whole before drying.

- The drying rack must be appropriately ventilated too to permit uniform drying. You can ensure constant ventilation by laying them out on a specialty drying mat or a screen.

- When you hang them out to dry, do not expose them to the direct glare of the sun lest you damage the nutrients

Drying will help to remove all moisture from the plants. They must be thoroughly dried before storing them lest they become growth media or bacteria and mold. You will know they are entirely dried if they become crumbly and brittle.

Once they are dried, transfer them into air-tight containers, freezer bags, or mason jars. Do not forget to label each of these containers and include the label's storage date. Some of the species of wild edible plants you can dry are morels and lobster mushrooms, including yarrow, jack pine, mint, red clover, strawberry, raspberry, etc.

You may be thinking how you would preserve the delicacy to enjoy it throughout the summer since eating fresh wild items is daunting during the winter. By storing your harvest in a variety of methods, you may take advantage of nature's abundance even during the chilly months:

- Blanching and Freezing Food

- Drying Food

Blanching and Freezing Food

Researching which wild delicacies, like lamb's quarters, need to be blanched before freezing is recommended. Others may be frozen as is. The simplest way to store your produce is by freezing it. Chop the plants after giving them a short rinse in freezing water and shaking off the extra water. Freeze the plants in ice cube trays. When frozen, store plant cubes in freezer bags or airtight plastic containers. Wild edibles may also be frozen on a baking sheet. Once frozen, put wild foods in a freezer bag. When thawed, wild foods cannot be used in salads but may be cooked. Refreeze after thawing.

Drying Food

Traditional plant preservation involves drying. Clean wild foods should not be dampened. Rattle off excess water, rinse the leaves to remove dust and dirt, and remove dead or damaged foliage.

Wrap the stems in twine or elastic bands and hang them upside-down in a warm, dry, airy spot indoors or outdoors, but not in direct sunlight. Bundle products loosely to allow air movement. The ideal technique is to use elastic bands, as they adjust to the stems' size as they dry and lose moisture. Bundles may be strung using paperclips.

Many plants discolor and lose taste due to UV radiation from the sun and moisture from rain and frost. Herbs should be dried in a closet, attic, or unused room corner. Dried herbs give an area a pleasant organic fragrance.

Instead of hanging plants to dry, lay them out on a clean window screen or build your own. Chair backs may support window screens; ventilation is key. Turn leaves regularly to ensure even drying.

Drying wild foods in a regular oven is possible. The plant should be dried on a baking sheet and placed in the oven at the lowest temperature possible. Dehydrators that are used in the home are also efficient. Wild foods that have been dried out tend to be brittle and crumbly. Remove the leaves off the stalks when they have dried out (unless the stem possesses nutritional value). When preserving dried plants, Mason jars with secure lids are the way to go. You might also use sturdy plastic bags with zip-lock closures.

Wild foods that have been dried should be maintained in a cool, dry place away of the sun, humidity, and heat. If maintained appropriately, the normal shelf life is one to two years. Dried wild foods improve the flavor and nutritious content of soups, stews, potato dishes, and pancakes.

Canning, Preserving, and Bottling

Check the Operating Guidelines for Home Caning before you can edible wild food. Use only new jars and lids for caning and bottling. The risk of botulism is lower in foods rich in acid and can, therefore, be canned. The reverse is the case in foods with low acid contents. Never forget to label the canned or bottled foods for future reference.

How To Prepare A Selection of Wild Foods

Asparagus (Asparagus officinalis)

This vegetable grows wild throughout Europe, North Africa, West Asia, and North America. Wild asparagus is thinner than store-bought. It contains vitamin C, thiamine, potassium, and B6. Like asparagus, you can eat it raw or boiled.

Purslane (Portulaca oleracea)

Purslane is an invasive plant in the U.S., yet it might give vitamins and minerals in a survival circumstance. It is a little, luxuriant shrub with velvety, sour leaves. From June until October, purslane blossoms and is excellent fresh or cooked. It can also be boiled to eradicate the sour flavor from the leaves.

Burdock (Arctium lappa)

Large plant with huge leaves and thistle-like purple flowers. The plant is endemic to the temperate Eastern Hemisphere but has naturalized in the Western. In Japan, burdock is also a common dish. You may consume the raw or boiling leaves and stems. However, to eliminate the bitterness from the leaves, boil them twice. Roots may be peeled, cooked, and eaten too.

Clovers (Trifolium)

Clovers are human-safe. They are common in grassy open spaces. Their leaves have trefoil-shaped leaflets. Clovers taste better boiling than raw.

Dandelion (Taraxacum officinale)

This weedy shrub may be a lifeline in the woods. The plant's roots, leaves, and blossom are all edible. Young leaves are sweeter than adult ones. Boiling ripe leaves removes their harsh flavor. Before eating, boil the roots. You may use the cooked roots to make tea and the bloom to garnish dandelion salad.

Curled Dock (Rumex crispus)

Australia, Europe, North America, and South America have curved dock. It has a long, brilliant red stem that may grow to three feet. Raw or cooked stalk is edible. Remove the top layer, eliminate the leaves' harsh flavor, and boil them in multiple changes of water.

Field Pennycress (Thalspi vulgaris)

Field pennycress is found worldwide during early spring until late winter. Field pennycress seeds and leaves may be consumed uncooked or cooked. Field pennycress grown in polluted soil should never be eaten. As a chelating agent, they may absorb all the minerals in its surroundings. Those growing near a Superfund site should not be eaten

Cattail (Typha)

The typha genus of plants is often found around freshwater marshes in North America and England. Rootstocks may be boiled or eaten raw and can be acquired underground. The white section of the stem is the finest, which can be consumed either boiled or uncooked. If the plant is young, the female flower spike may be eaten like corn on the cob and its corn flavored if you encounter challenges with identifying the plant.

Chicory (Cichorium intybus)

Chicory is a European plant that grows in North America and Australia. Its thick shrub bears blue, lavender, and white blooms. Consume the entire plant. Eat fresh, still-on-the-plant leaves raw or cooked. Cooked chicory roots taste better. Chewing on the blooms is another option.

White Mustard (Synapsis alba)

The wild form of white mustard may be found in many distinct parts of the world. The flowering period lasts from February through March. You are allowed to ingest the plant's seeds as well as its flowers and leaves.

Green Seaweed (Ulva lactuca)

If you are shipwrecked, look for green seaweed. This substance may be in global water. After removing green seaweed from water, rinse and dry it. Fresh or cooked, it is versatile. If you are feeling daring, grab a fish with your homemade spear and create sushi rolls using seaweed instead of rice.

Kelp (Alaria esculenta)

One kind of seaweed is called kelp. It is obtainable in most the world's areas. Consume it uncooked or include it into a broth dish. Kelp has a high concentration of lignans, folate, and vitamin K.

Example Recipes for Preparing Wild Plants

Amaranth (Amaranthus retroflexus and other species)

Amaranth is a global edible weed native to the Americas. You may consume all the plant components but beware of the spines on certain leaves. Amaranth leaves contain oxalic acid and, if cultivated on nitrate-rich soil, nitrates. To eliminate oxalic acid and nitrates, boil the leaves. Do not consume plant-boiling water. If necessary, the leaves may be eaten uncooked.

Ingredients

- Three cups of water

- One cup Amaranth

Instructions

- Add 3 cups of water to a strong bottom pan

- Bring it to a boil

- Add 1 cup of dry amaranth seeds

- Give it a stir

- Close the lid and let it cook on low heat

- Simmer until the water has been absorbed for about 20 minutes

Wood Sorrel (Oxalis)

South America has the most kinds of wood sorrel. Millennia ago, humans used wood sorrel for food and medicine. Kiowa Native Americans chewed wood sorrel to reduce thirst and Cherokee to repair mouth sores which are Vitamin C-rich leaves. Wood sorrel roots are sometimes boiled. Like potatoes, they are starchy and flavorful.

Ingredients

- 3 tbsps. unsalted butter

- 1/2 cup finely chopped shallots or onions

- 4 to 6 cups of chopped garden and wood sorrel, packed

- 1 liter vegetable stock

- 1/2 cup cream

- pinch of salt

Instructions

- Melt butter in a soup pot. Add the onions and turn the heat to medium-low. Sauté. Pour the stock into the pot and bring to a simmer.

- Turn the heat back to medium, add the sorrel leaves and a healthy pinch of salt and stir well. When the sorrel is mostly wilted, turn the heat back to low. Cover and cook 10 minutes. Stir occasionally.

- To finish the soup, whisk in the cream and let simmer on extremely low for 5 minutes.

- Serve at once. Alternatively, this soup can be enjoyed cold as well.

Sheep Sorrel (Rumex acetosella)

Sheep sorrel is native to Europe and Asia but has become widespread in the United States. In woodlands, meadows, and fields. It prefers acidic soil. Sheep sorrel has a reddish-brown, 18-inch stem. Sheep sorrel is strong in oxalates, so do not eat too much. Uncooked leaves are edible. They have a lemon-like sour taste.

Ingredients

- Four tablespoons unsalted butter, divided

- 1/2 cup chopped green onions, ramps, or other wild onion

- 4 cups of chopped sorrel, packed

- Salt

- Three tablespoons flour

- One quart chicken stock or vegetable stock

- Two egg yolks

- 1/2 cup cream

Instructions

- Melt three tablespoons butter in a soup pot. Turn heat to medium-low and add ramps. Cook 10 minutes covered.

- While the onions fry, boil the stock.

- Turn the heat, add the sorrel leaves and salt, and whisk thoroughly. Turn heat to medium-low, cover, and cook sorrel for 10 minutes. Infrequently stir. Flour 3 minutes over medium heat.

- Stir in heated stock. Simmer.

- Egg yolks and cream conclude the soup. Ladle soup into the egg-cream mixture while whisking it. Repetition. Whisk soup. Whisk hot egg-cream-soup mixture into soup pot. Add remaining butter.

Fireweed (Epilobium angustifolium)

Most low-growing shrubs grow in the Northern Hemisphere. Fireweed is readily identified by its purple flowers and circular leaf veins, which do not end at the leaf margins. Native American foods included fireweed. Consume the leaves when they are delicate and fresh. Mature fireweed plants have stiff, astringent leaves. Humans may swallow the plant's stem and the spicy blooms and seeds. Fireweed is rich in A and C.

Ingredients

- fresh fireweed leaves

Instructions

- Cut fireweed stalks just below the last attractive leaf; lower on the plant, the leaves become scraggly. Put the leaves in a basin.

- Roll some leaves in your hands. You should bruise the leaves by rolling them tightly. bruised rolls in a lidded container.

- When all the fireweed is rolled and bruised, cover the container and store at room temperature. Move the leaves once or twice a day throughout the 2-to-3-day fermentation. You want a damp climate, but not so humid that the leaves mold. Watch it. Remove moldy leaves.

- After two to three days, if you live in a hot, dry region, put the leaves out in the sun to dry. Steaming the leaves for 5 minutes or roasting them at 350F for 20 minutes may also halt fermentation. Sun-drying and steaming are my favorites. A steam bath followed by sun drying creates the greatest tea.

- Keep tea in a cold, dry Mason jar. A silica packet prevents mold. This preserves tea for 2 years.

- Brew as loose-leaf black tea.

Chickweed (Stellaria media)

This plant grows well in both warm and freezing conditions. The leaves are big, and the shrub is sometimes covered with small white flowers. They are most common during the months of May and July. Humans may eat either the raw or cooked leaves. The leaves are rich in a vitamins and minerals

Ingredients

- 1 Cup of Tahini

- 1 Tbsp Olive Oil

- 1 Cup Lemon Juice

- 1 tsp Ground Cumin

- 1 Clove Minced Garlic

- 2 Cups drained Chickpeas

- 1 Cup Chickweed chopped

Ingredients

- add the tahini and lemon juice. Blend for 1 minute.

- Add the oil, cumin, salt, and garlic. Process for another minute.

- Add the chickpeas. Process for another minute. Add the chickweed and process until smooth.

- Add the water until the desired thickness is reached.

- Store in the refrigerator

Plantain (Plantago)

Plantain (not to be confused with banana-like plantain) has been used as food and used medicinally for millennia. Plantains thrive in marshes, bogs, and alpine areas. The ovate leaves have tiny stalks so they may lay low. Leaves may be six inches long and four inches wide. Fresh leaves are best. As the plant develops, the leaves become astringent. Plantain contains vitamin A and calcium. It includes vitamin C.

Ingredients

- tablespoons fresh plantain leaves (rinsed) or 2 teaspoons dried plantain leaves

- A cup of boiling water

Instructions

- Boil the leaves for 10 minutes.

- After straining, sweeten with honey, maple syrup, or another sweetener.

Prickly Pear Cactus (Opuntia)

The pleasant and healthful prickly pear cactus, endemic to North American deserts, might save your life if you get lost. Prickly pear cactus fruit is crimson or reddish. The name follows. If you eat the plant without removing its spines, you may feel like you are eating a porcupine. Young cactus stems may be eaten. Boil stems before eating.

Ingredients

- Peeled prickly pears.

- A cup of water

- A cup of thyme honey

- An inch of cinnamon stick

- cup of lemon juice

Instructions

- Rinse the cacti. Peel latex gloves.

- Break them with a potato masher in water. Boil and remove immediately. Cool.

- Press them in a colander over a basin to remove the juice.

- Juice, honey, geranium leaves, and cinnamon. Melt the honey overheat. Simmer for 15 minutes after boiling.

- Cool. If not thick enough, boil again. Five minutes more. Turn off the heat after adding lemon juice.

- Remove cinnamon stick and geranium leaves, then store in sterilized jars.

- Serve with Greek yogurt, pancakes, crepes, ice cream, moist sponge cakes, etc.

100+ Quick and Easy Recipes

1. Bittercress

Ingredients:

- 2 tsp. of olive oil
- 1 bunch of bittercress
- ½ tsp. red chili flakes
- Kosher salt and pepper
- 3 cloves of garlic
- 1 small onion, minced

Preparation:

1. Heat the oil in a saucepan on low heat. Add the red crushed chili flakes, garlic, and onion. Continue cooking until you perceive the aroma.
2. Add the bittercress and increase the heat.
3. Continue stirring until the bittercress wilts and add salt.
4. Serve with vegetables or meat.

2. Black-Eyed Susan Cocktail

Ingredients:

- 2 oz. orange juice
- 1 oz. peach schnapps
- 1 oz. vodka
- 1 oz. bourbon whiskey
- 2 oz. sour milk
- Cherry to garnish
- Orange slice to garnish

Preparation:

1. Fill a cocktail shaker with ice. Pour the peach schnapps, vodka, bourbon, sour mix, and orange juice. Shake it very well.
2. Pour crushed ice into a tall glass and pour the mixture over the crushed ice into the glass.
3. Add the cherry and orange to garnish.

3. Burdock

Ingredients:

- 2 tbsp. sugar
- 1 tbsp. sake
- 2 tbsp. soy sauce
- 1 tbsp. fat or cooking oil
- 2 burdock roots about 1 foot long

Preparation:

1. Wash the burdock root and peel it. Cut it into pieces, 4-inch length each. Quarter each of them longitudinally and place in an ice water bath, adding a splash of vinegar to it.
2. Prepare a sauté pan and place it over medium heat. Add oil to the pan and sauté the burdock root for about 6 minutes until it becomes light brown.
3. Add the sugar, soy sauce, and sake. Allow simmering for about 5 minutes until it cooks. You can serve cold or at room temperature.

4. Caramelized Chicory with Orange and Thyme

Ingredients:

- 1 tbsp. cider or sherry vinegar
- 1 tbsp. clear honey
- 1 orange zested and juiced orange
- Few sprigs of fresh thyme
- 8 peeled garlic cloves
- 2 x 270g of packed chicory

Preparation:

1. Heat the oven to 180°C.
2. Cover the interior of a roasting tin with grease.
3. Divide the chicory in half or leave it whole if it is smaller. Arrange them in the dish and add the garlic to the chicory. Add black pepper and thyme sprigs to season.
4. Pour one tablespoon of orange juice, vinegar, and honey into the pan. You can also add butter to it and bake it in the oven.
5. Leave it for about an hour and turn the chicory about 3 times while baking.
6. Add the orange zest and leave it for another 15 minutes to cook.

5. Chickichurri (Chickweed)

Ingredients:

- ½ c. finely chopped chickweed
- ½ tbsp. chopped fresh oregano
- 3 cloves of finely minced garlic
- 2 tbsp. red wine vinegar
- 1 small jalapeno
- 1 tbsp. Sea salt
- ½ c. olive oil
- ½ tbsp. freshly ground black pepper
- Half large finely chopped shallot

Preparation:

1. Chop the herbs and place them in the oven.
2. Mix each ingredient and add to the herbs.
3. Allow cooking for about 10 minutes.

6. Claytonia and Arugula Salad (Claytonia)

Ingredients:

- 1 c. claytonia leaves
- Salt and pepper to taste
- 2 tbsp. vinegar
- 6 tbsp. olive oil
- ½ c. toasted nuts
- 1 c. green apple
- 2 c. chopped arugula

Preparation:

1. Add the greens into a single bowl.
2. Add the nuts and apples to the greens in the bowl.
3. Add pepper, salt, vinegar, and oil to another container and mix.
4. Drizzle the sauce over the salad and serve.

7.   Cleaver Juice (Cleaver)

Ingredients:

- 1 tbsp. xylitol
- 1 lemon
- 2 large handfuls of cleavers

Preparation:

1. Pour the xylitol, lemon, and cleavers into a container.
2. Add water to it and place it in a refrigerator for about 1 week.
3. Strain the extra liquid and transfer it into an air-tight container.
4. Add sparkling water to it and mix. You can also add vodka as a form of refreshment.

8. White Clover Pudding (Clover)

Ingredients:

- 2 c. white clover blossoms
- 1 c. water
- 1 tbsp. organic unflavored gelatin
- ½ c. fresh orange juice
- 1 c. stiff heavy cream

- 4 tbsp. white clover honey
- Pinch of salt

Preparation:

1. Add the gelatin to a quarter cup of water to dissolve.
2. Pour the white clover blossoms into a small saucepan and place them on a low heat to boil. Add salt, honey, orange juice, and water to it.
3. Turn off the heat and continue stirring the gelatin to dissolve completely. Then leave it for about 10 minutes.
4. Cover and place in the fridge to allow the gelatin to firm.
5. Add heavy cream and mix until the mixture becomes stiff.
6. Place it into a serving bowl and return to the fridge to allow it to set.

9. Comfrey Plantain Salve (Comfrey)

Ingredients:

- Rosemary essential oil
- 4 tsp. beeswax pastilles
- 1 ½ c. olive oil
- ½ c. dry plantain leaves
- ½ c. dry comfrey leaves

Preparation:

1. Make an infusion using dried herbs and olive oil.
2. Strain the infused oil by pouring it through fine-mesh cheesecloth and into a mason jar.
3. Add the beeswax pastilles and continue stirring until it all melts.
4. After melted, add 20 drops of the rosemary essential oil and mix thoroughly.
5. Pour everything into a container, ready to use.

10. Wild Curly Dock Masala (Curly Dock)

Ingredients:

- ½ c. onion

- ¼ c. fresh coriander leaves
- ½ tbsp. pan-toasted mustard seeds
- 4 c. curly dock leaves, de-stemmed and washed
- 2 tsp. Freshly grated ginger
- ½ tsp. salt to taste
- 4 tsp. homemade gram masala
- 2 c. coconut milk

Preparation:

1. Pour all the ingredients into a dry pan before grinding the mustard seeds.
2. Add the masala and mix until evenly combined. Add salt to taste
3. Add the curly dock, coating it with the aromatics and spice mixture.
4. Cool and blend until it appears smooth. It is now ready for serving.

11. Dandelion Greens with a Kick (Dandelion)

Ingredients:

- Half thinly sliced onion
- 1 tbsp. butter
- 2 tbsp. olive oil
- 1 tsp. salt
- 1 pound of dandelion greens
- 1 tbsp. grated parmesan cheese
- Salt and ground black pepper to taste
- 2 cloves of minced garlic
- ¼ tsp. red pepper flakes

Preparation:

1. Soak the herbs in a big bowl containing cold water and add one teaspoon of salt. Leave for 10 minutes.
2. Place a large pot of water on heat to boil. Let the greens cook until they become tender, then drain and rinse using cold water.

3. Heat the butter and olive oil in a large skillet on medium heat. Add the red pepper and onion and stir until they become tender. This should take about 30 minutes. Increase the heat to medium-high and pour in the dandelion greens. Let it cook until the liquid evaporates. Add black pepper and salt to season.

4. Put the parmesan cheese to serve.

12. Garlic Mustard Pesto

Ingredients:

- 11 c. packed garlic mustard leaves
- 2 squeezes of lemon juice
- ½ tsp. sugar
- ½ tsp. salt
- 12 c. extra virgin olive oil
- ⅓ c. grated parmesan cheese
- 1 garlic clove
- ¼ c. pine nuts

Preparation:

1. Pour the parmesan, pine nuts, and garlic into a blender and blend.
2. Add the garlic mustard.
3. Pour the olive oil steadily for about 1 minute into the blender and continue blending until the mixture is smooth.
4. Add lemon juice, sugar, pulse, and salt until they are well mixed.
5. Serve and enjoy.

13. Henbit Salad

Ingredients:

- 4 c. Henbit shoots
- 3 tbsp. butter
- 1 tsp. curry powder
- 2 whole cloves

- ¼ tsp. ground cinnamon
- 2 tbsp. flour
- 3 c. sour cream

Preparation:

1. Chop four cups of henbit.
2. Pour into a pot and cover with water.
3. Place on a stove and let it boil for about 10 minutes.
4. Add the butter to another pan and add the ground cinnamon, cloves, and curry powder. Stir and allow to cook for 1 minute.
5. Add boiling water to the henbit and continue stirring until it becomes smooth.
6. Drain and pour the boiled henbit together with 3 cups of sour cream.
7. Let it cook for another 15 minutes and serve.

14. Herb Robert Tea

Ingredients:

- 2 L of ginger ale
- ¼ c. honey
- ¼ c. orange juice
- ¼ c. lemon juice
- ¼ c. finely chopped fresh mint
- ¼ c. finely chopped lemon balm

Preparation:

1. Add the five ingredients into a small bowl.
2. Allow steeping for 1 hour.
3. Strain it and remove the herbs from the mixture.
4. Pour the tea into a pitcher.
5. Add the ginger ale and stir before you serve.

15. Himalayan Balsam Curry

Ingredients:

- Himalayan balsam seed
- 1 onion
- Olive oil
- 1 swede
- 2 tbsp. Curry paste
- 2 sticks of celery
- 2 tomatoes
- 2 red pepper

Preparation:

1. Slice the onion and pour it into a pan. Pour the olive oil into a pan.
2. Add the sliced onion and fry gently until it becomes translucent.
3. Cut the swede into small cubes and pour into a bowl.
4. Add the curry paste to the mixture on the stove and mix. Allow everything to fry for 1 minute.
5. After 1 minute, add the Himalayan balsam and stir.
6. Add the swede to the mixture on the stove. Add hot water to cover the saucepan.
7. Add the sticks of celery and creamed coconut.
8. Chop the tomatoes and add to the pan. Slice the red pepper thinly and also add.
9. Allow simmering until the vegetables become tender. Serve and enjoy.

16. Horsetail Tea

Ingredients:

- Honey or sweetener of your choice
- 2 c. hot water
- 3 tsp. dried horsetail

Preparation:

1. Pour water into a pot and bring to boil on a stove.
2. Add the dried horsetail to a teapot.
3. Pour the hot water on the horsetail.
4. Leave the tea to steep for about 10 minutes.
5. Strain the tea and add honey or any sweetener you prefer. Enjoy the tea.

17. Japanese Knotweed

Ingredients:

- 2 tbsp. butter
- 1 ½ oz. finely chopped Japanese Knotweed
- Salt to taste

Preparation:

1. Pour the butter into a skillet and melt it on medium-high heat.

2. Lower the heat to medium and pour the Japanese Knotweed when it has foamed.

3. Allow it to cook for about 10 minutes and stir a few times while it cooks.

4. You will see it lose its crunch as it turns khaki color. Add salt and serve.

18. Jewelweed Tincture (Jewelweed)

Ingredients:

- Crockpot
- Witch hazel
- Fresh jewelweed
- 1 quart jar

Preparation:

1. Chop the jewelweed plant and pour it into the quart jar. Cover with witch hazel and close.

2. Transfer the jar to the Crockpot and add water as high as possible without covering the neck of the jar.

3. Set the heat to low/warm.

4. Place a towel over the Crockpot if the jar is too tall.

5. Leave it for about 48 hours.

6. Strain it and transfer it to a cool dark place. You can now spray on any infected area or dab it with cotton balls.

19. Deep Fried Kudzu Tofu (Kudzu)

Ingredients:

- 4 g thin spring onion
- ½ c. mentsuyu
- 1 tbsp. potatoes starch
- 20 g kudzu starch
- 250mls of soymilk

Preparation:

1. Pour the kudzu starch and soymilk into a bowl and mix. Then pour into a sauce pot and cook on low flame. Stir as you cook.
2. Transfer into a vat and then into a fridge. Allow it to firm in the refrigerator.
3. Cut the tofu into four pieces and sprinkle potato starch over it.
4. Add a small quantity of oil into a pan to fry the tofu. Flip over to the other side once one side browns.
5. Serve and garnish with green onions.

20. Lady's Thumb Salad

Ingredients:

- Raw uncooked lady's thumb leaves
- Sour Cream
- A couple of fruits, depending on which you like

Preparation:

1. Chop the lady's thumb leaves and pour them into a bowl.
2. Chop the fruits also and add them to the bowl.
3. Spread the sour milk on it and enjoy.

21. Creamy Lambs Quarter Gratin

Ingredients:

- 1 ½ pounds' lambs-quarters
- 1 bunch of chopped scallions
- Salt
- 1 tbsp. olive oil
- 1 c. milk
- Freshly ground black pepper
- 3 tbsp. unsalted butter
- 3 tbsp. All-purpose flour
- ¼ tsp. nutmeg

Preparation:

1. Heat the oven to 350°F and place the rack in the middle.
2. Boil slated water in a large saucepan. Also, wash the lamb's quarters in a bowl using cold water and drain.
3. Cook the lambs' quarter on medium heat until the stems are tender and the leaves are wilted.
4. Drain the greens and rinse well using running cold water. Press out the excess liquid.
5. Once done, chop the greens and pour them into a bowl.
6. Pour the scallion into olive oil and cook, adding a quarter teaspoon of salt.
7. Melt the butter for 2 minutes.
8. Mix the sauce into the green mixture and spread it out in a baking dish.

22. Andalusian Mallow with Chickpea (Mallow Species)

Ingredients:

- 4 tsp. cumin seeds
- A bagful of mallow leaves
- ½ bulb of crushed garlic
- A large jar of drained chickpeas
- Juice of a lemon
- Salt to taste
- Olive oil

Preparation:

1. Rinse the mallow leaves and slice roughly.
2. Add leaves to a pan containing water and steam on low heat.
3. Pour the cumin seeds into a large frying pan and dry toast it. Grind in a grinder.
4. Fry the cumin using olive oil on medium heat, add the garlic, and stir.
5. Add the chickpea and stir in the mellow. Let it cook for about 15 minutes and add water if it dries up.
6. Add lemon juice and salt to taste, and then serve.

23. Melilot Blancmange

Ingredients:

- 2 c. whole milk
- ⅛ c. dried melilot
- ¼ c. cornstarch
- 3 tbsp. sugar

Preparation:

1. Crumble the melilot and pour it into a pint jar.
2. Fill the jar with the milk and cover it.
3. Shake well and put in the refrigerator for about 5 hours.
4. Strain the milk and throw away the solids.
5. Pour the milk into a saucepan. Add the sugar and cornstarch. Place on a stove to heat the mixture and whisk to dissolve the solids.
6. Remove when it starts boiling and serve.

24. Mugwort Soup

Ingredients:

- 3 tbsp. unsalted butter
- 1 medium onion
- 1 large Yukon gold
- 10 medium white mushrooms
- 2 cloves of minced garlic
- Coarse salt
- Tobacco
- 4 oz. tender mugwort
- 1 c. heavy cream
- 6 c. low-sodium chicken

Preparation:

1. Add the butter to a pot and place it over medium heat to melt. Add the onion and allow it to sauté until it softens. Add the mushroom and garlic and cook until they soften.
2. Add potatoes and broth. Then allow boiling.
3. Lower heat and simmer for about 20 minutes.

4. Add the mugwort and cream and allow simmering for 10 minutes. Remove from heat and let cool.

5. Puree in batches using a blender and return to the pot.

6. Add adequate Tabasco to taste. Then add pepper and salt.

25. Mullein Tea

Ingredients:

- 2 tsp. dried mullein leaves

Preparation:

1. Pour water over the dried mullein leaves. You can also use flowers.

2. Allow it to steep for about 15 minutes.

3. Serve and drink.

26. Pigweed Smoothie (Pigweed)

Ingredients:

- 1 c. coconut water
- Honey or 3 dates as a sweetener
- 1 tbsp. chia seeds
- Half a pear
- Half an apple
- A handful of spinach and pigweed mix

Preparation:

1. Pour the greens into the blender and add coconut water. Then blend until the leaves liquefy.

2. Add the remaining ingredients and blend again until smooth.

3. Serve and enjoy.

27. Pineapple Weed Tea

Ingredients:

- A handful of pineapple weed heads

- Honey or sugar to taste

Preparation:

1. Add the pineapple weed into a teapot.
2. Pour boiling water on it and let it steep for 5 minutes.
3. Pour the tea into a mug or cup.
4. Add honey or sugar to taste.

28. Plantain Tea

Ingredients:

- 1 c. boiling water
- 3 tbsp. fresh plantain leaves

Preparation:

1. Boil some water and pour it on the leaves. Allow infusing for about 10 minutes.
2. Strain the leaves and add sweeteners, like maple syrup, honey, or another sweetener.
3. Serve and enjoy.

29. Purple Dead-Nettle Salve

Ingredients:

- 7 g beeswax
- 47 g purple dead nettle infused oil
- 3 drips of lavender essential oil

Preparation:

1. Add the beeswax and infused oil to a heatproof jar.
2. Pour some water into a saucepan and place the jar in the water. This will form a double boiler.
3. Allow melting by heating over medium-low heat.
4. Add lavender to it and remove it from the heat source.
5. Melt entirely on medium heat.
6. Pour it into 2 glass jars.
7. Allow it to cool and serve to eat.

30. Steamed Purslane

Ingredients:

- 2 c. purslane
- Salt and pepper to taste
- 2 tbsp. Cotija cheese
- 1 tbsp. olive oil
- 1 clove of garlic

Preparation:

1. Add a cup of water to a small saucepan. Add the garlic cloves.
2. Place on medium-high heat and allow the water to boil.
3. Add the purslane. Lower the heat and cover the saucepan. Allow it to cook for about 6 minutes.
4. Remove from heat and drain. You can now add olive oil, salt, and pepper. Add the Cotija cheese when serving.

31. Queen Anne's Lace Cognac Cocktail

Ingredients:

- 1 ½ tbsp. fine sugar
- 3 tbsp. dried Queen Anne's lace fruits
- 2 oz. Cognac
- ¾ oz. honey syrup
- ¾ oz. fresh Meyer lemon juice
- 1 tsp. dried Queen Anne's lace fruit

Preparation:

1. Add sugar to the Queen Anne's Lace fruits and crush them, followed by thorough mixing.
2. Pour the mixture on a plate or saucer larger than a glass rim in diameter.
3. Moisten the glass rim with water, then dip the moistened rim in the mixture and firmly press it down.
4. Shake off the excess.
5. Add lemon juice syrup, cognac, and ice to a cocktail shaker.
6. Shake it well for about 30 minutes.
7. Pour the mixture through a strainer and into a rimmed glass.
8. Serve immediately.

32. Quick Weed Potato Salad

Ingredients:

- 4 medium potatoes
- A couple of arugula leaves
- 2 c. quick weed or French weed leaves
- 6 slices of hard salami
- 1 spring of finely sliced onion
- 1 minced garlic
- A third walnut oil
- 1 tbsp. capers
- ⅓ c. chopped walnut

Preparation:

1. Rinse and cut the potatoes, and boil for 20 minutes.
2. Cool after draining.
3. Cut the salami and slice the onion. Then add the quick weed. Sauté for some minutes.
4. Gather all the ingredients in a big bowl. Add chopped walnuts, capers, pepper, and salt to taste. Then add walnut oil and mix gently.
5. Place in the fridge to cool for about an hour, and then serve. You can add arugula leaves when serving.

33. Self-Heal Skin Serum

Ingredients:

- 5 oz. jojoba oil
- 1 oz. pomegranate oil
- 4 oz. argon oil
- 1 tsp. rosemary extract
- 15 g dried self-heal herb
- 3 drops of blue chamomile essential oil
- 7 drops of lavender essential oil
- 20 drops of neroli essential oil
- 1 tsp. rosemary extract

Preparation:

1. Add the pomegranate oil, argan oil, and jojoba oil into a double boiler.
2. Add about 15 g to the self-heal herb.
3. Warm in the double boiler and turn off the heat.
4. Let it cool for about 48 hours and transfer to a blender. Blend until it is warm.
5. Strain the herb from the oil, and the oil will take on a deep dark green color.
6. Add the essential oil and rosemary extract.
7. Put the oil in a bottle or traditional tincture.

34. Shepherd's Purse Soup

Ingredients:

- 8 oz. frozen shepherd purse
- 3 eggs whites
- ¼ cornstarch
- ¼ tsp. ground white pepper
- 1 tsp. sesame oil
- 1 ½ tsp. salt
- 4 c. homemade chicken stock

- Half block of silken tofu

Preparation:

1. Thaw the shepherd's purse. After, squeeze out the water in it and chop the leaves.
2. Cut the tofu into half cubes.
3. Heat the chicken stock in a medium pot, then add salt, ground white pepper, and sesame oil.
4. Add cornstarch and water, and then mix. Reduce the heat and drizzle the cornstarch slurry slowly into the soup. Continue stirring.
5. Turn on the heat as you stir. Add salt to taste too.
6. Allow the soup to simmer for a minute.
7. Add the tofu cubes and stir. Allow the soup to simmer for about 4 minutes and add cornstarch slurry if you want the soup to be thicker.

35. Speedwell Salad

Ingredients:

- Fresh Speedwell leaves
- Other fruits of your choosing
- Sour cream

Preparation:

1. Chop the speedwell leaves and the fruits.
2. Transfer to a bowl and spread the sour cream on it.
3. Serve and enjoy.

36. St. John's Wort Oil

Ingredients:

- Aerial part of Fresh St. John's wort
- 1 sterilized quart-sized canning jar with a lid
- Organic extra virgin olive oil

Preparation:

1. Place the fresh flowers and buds in a canning jar and fill with ¾ of fresh herbs.
2. Add the extra virgin olive oil until it covers the herbs by an inch and covers the jar.
3. Place the mixture for three weeks on a sunny windowsill.
4. Strain the oil when it runs deep red and pour it into an amber-colored glass bottle.
5. Place the oil in a cool dark place for storage.

37. Garlicky Nettles Pesto

Ingredients:

- ⅓ c. grated parmesan cheese
- 1 ¼ c. extra virgin olive oil
- 1 tbsp. freshly squeezed lemon juice
- Freshly ground pepper
- ½ tsp. salt
- ½ c. toasted pine nuts
- 4 large, smashed garlic cloves
- Half pound of nettle

Preparation:

1. Pour water into a pot and add salt. Place on the stove and allow simmering.
2. Add the nettle to the pot and cook for about 2 minutes.
3. Drain the herb and allow it to cool.
4. Wrap the nettle in a dishtowel and wring out the moisture.
5. Grind the garlic, pine nuts, pepper, and salt until they are fine.
6. Add oil and continue mixing until it becomes smooth.

7. Then add the cheese and seasoning to taste.

38. Thistle

Ingredients:

- Thistle leaves and stems
- Tomato paste
- Glug of honey

Preparation:

1. Remove the edge from the leaves and put the ribs to the side.
2. Remove the thorns using a vegetable peeler.
3. Blanch the stems and ribs.
4. Pour the olive oil into a pan and pour the chili powder to heat.
5. Pour the tomato paste into it and also add a cup of water.
6. Pour the thistle and continue simmering until the ribs become soft.
7. Remove the heat and add honey.
8. Serve over rice and enjoy.

39. Valerian Tea

Ingredients:

- Valerian root

Preparation:

1. Boil some water and pour the valerian root into it.
2. After boiling, allow the leaves to steep.
3. Serve and enjoy.

40. Orange and Viola Infused Water

Ingredients:

- ½ c. violet
- 2 large, peeled and sliced oranges
- 1 gallon of cold water
- 4 c. of ice cubes

Preparation:

1. Clean the violet flower to remove insects and other contaminants.
2. Dry by placing absorbent paper on them.
3. Add ice cubes to the liquid and serve with orange slices.

41. Sauteed Watercress with Garlic

Ingredients:

- 2 tbsp. olive oil
- 2 bunches of rinsed and trimmed watercress
- 6 minced and grated garlic cloves

Preparation:

1. Pour the oil into a skillet and put it on medium heat. Add the garlic and sauté until it gives out a fragrance.
2. Add the watercress and salt. Allow to cook and stir while cooking for about 40 seconds.
3. Add two tablespoons of water and stir again until the leaves wilt.

42. Chilled Lemony Wood Sorrel Soup

Ingredients:

- 2 cloves of minced garlic
- Olive oil
- 1 c. full-fat coconut milk
- 3 medium-sized mint leaves
- 2 c. lightly packed wood sorrel
- 2 c. of vegetable broth
- 2 chopped scallions
- Pepper and salt to taste

Preparation:

1. Pour the olive oil into a small saucepan
2. Sauté the garlic until it starts producing fragrance, and then add scallions.
3. Cover the garlic with vegetable broth and boil.
4. Allow it to simmer for about 5 minutes, after which you can add sorrel for about 30 seconds
5. Remove from heat and add mint. Then blend smoothly
6. Add the coconut milk, salt, and pepper.
7. Place in the refrigerator until chilled. Serve and enjoy.

43. Wild Bergamot Tea

Ingredients:

- Bergamot herb
- Sweetener of your choice

Preparation:

1. Boil some water and pour on the bergamot herb.
2. Allow it to seep and pour into a teacup.
3. Serve and add sweetener.

44. Wild Lettuce Tea

Ingredients:

- Lettuce leaves
- Any sweetener

Preparation:

1. Dry the wild lettuce leaves with low heat or a dehydrator.
2. Grind the leaves and add two teaspoons to a cup of water in a bowl.
3. Steep for about five minutes.
4. Strain the water and drink. You can add any sweetener of your choice.

45. Wild Mint Mojitos

Ingredients:

- White rum
- Soda water
- 1 tsp. sugar
- Lime juice
- Mint leaves
- Ice cubes
- Lemon slices for decoration

Preparation:

1. Put the lime juice, sugar, and mint in a glass until it starts releasing a flavor.
2. Add ice to the glass and pour some rum over it. Stir together.
3. Add soda water and mint leaves. Then add the lemon slice. Enjoy.

46. Yarrow Tea

Ingredients:

- 1 tsp. dried yarrow
- Slice of lemon
- 1 c. of boiling water

Preparation:

1. Pour boiling water into a mug and add dried yarrow to it.
2. Leave it for about ten minutes to steep.
3. Strain the leaves.
4. Add honey or lemon slices and enjoy.

47. Sweet and Sour Crabapple

Ingredients:

- 4 cinnamon sticks
- 3 pounds of crab apples
- 1 whole nutmeg
- 3 dozen of whole cloves
- 3 c. apple cider vinegar
- 3 c. water
- 2 ¼ c. sugar

Preparation:

1. Transfer all the ingredients to a large pot. Make a brine and add the spice bag. Place on the stove to cook for about three minutes.
2. Turn the stove to a lower temperature so that it can simmer and add the apple. Allow cooking for an additional 5 minutes.
3. Scoop the apple into a jar and pour the hot brine over it. Place a lid and band to secure.
4. Process it in a hot bath for about 20 minutes.

48. Arctic Raspberry

Ingredients:

- 2 large eggs
- 300g jar of raspberry jam
- 100g of punnet raspberry
- Seeds from a vanilla pod
- 350ml of whole milk
- 227g to tub clotted cream
- 140g of golden caster sugar

Preparation:

1. Whisk the eggs and sugar in a large bowl until they become fluffy and pale.
2. Add clotted cream, vanilla seeds, and milk, then whisk again.
3. Pour into a chilled ice cream maker and churn until it is frozen.
4. Add two tablespoons of jam to the raspberries.
5. Transfer to a tin and place in the freezer until solid. This can take about 6 hours or overnight.
6. Pour sugar and eggs into a large bowl and whisk for about 5 minutes. Spread it over the flour and fold until no lumps are visible.
7. Bake for about 12 minutes.
8. Serve and enjoy.

49. Aronia Berries Smoothie

Ingredients:

- ½ c. juiced arona berries
- Half a banana
- 2 tsp. lemon juice

Preparation:

1. Add sugar and water to the berries and boil on a stove.
2. Add pectin and lemon juice.
3. Allow cooling and serve.

50. Autumn Olive Jam

Ingredients:

- 7 ½ c. ripe autumn olive berries
- 2 under-ripe, unpeeled apples
- 2 c. sugar
- 3 c. water
- 1 ½ tbsp. lemon juice

Preparation:

1. Simmer the water, apples, and berries in a large pot for 15 minutes. Stir and mash the berries along.
2. Remove the apple peels and seeds, and they will produce about 4 cups of pulp or juice.
3. Add the pulp and juice to a large pot and add lemon juice and sugar.
4. Boil for about 20 minutes.
5. Pour it into a jar without filling it to the top.
6. Cover the jar and process in boiling water for about 15 minutes.

51. Pork Chops with Barberry (Barberry)

Ingredients:

- 3 c. water
- 6 bone-in center-cut pork loin chops
- 1 whole star anise pod
- 3 thyme sprigs
- 4 allspice berries
- 4 whole cloves
- 4 rosemary
- 1 ½ tbsp. honey
- 1 ½ tbsp. light brown
- 3 ½ tbsp. coarse sea salt

Preparation:

1. Add all the ingredients to a medium saucepan, leaving the pork chops.
2. Place on the stove to boil and stir to ensure the salt dissolves. Allow boiling for about 2 minutes.
3. Transfer to a medium bowl and pour ice water into another bowl.
4. Place the brine bowl in an ice bath until it gets cool. Make sure you also stir often.
5. Pour the brine into a bag and seal. Place the pork in a refrigerator for 2 hours.
6. Add the pomegranate juice, honey, and barberries into a medium saucepan.
7. Add the bay leaves, cloves, and thyme sprigs to the cheesecloth and tie them into a bundle.
8. Cover and simmer until it boils for 15 minutes.
9. Allow cooling and serve.

52. Bearberry Jelly (Bearberry)

Ingredients:

- 2 qt. berries
- 1 c. sugar per cup of juice
- 3 oz. of liquid pectin
- 1 tbsp. lemon juice

Preparation:

1. Make sure the berries are fully ripe. Wash and stem them. Then place them in a saucepan to cook until the fruit pops and the juice flows.
2. Turn off the heat and squeeze the berries through a jelly bag to extract the juice.
3. Measure the juice and pour it into a deep saucepan. Add the sugar and lemon juice, then mix very well.
4. Set the stove to high heat and boil the juice until all the sugar dissolves.
5. Add liquid pectin and boil for another 1 minute.
6. Skim off the foam and pour it into a sterile jar.

53. Mini Blackberry & Bay Pavlova's (Blackberry)

Ingredients:

- 2 fresh bay leaves
- 1 ½ tbsp. caster sugar
- 450g blackberries

Preparation:

1. Add the blackberries to a non-reactive pan. Add bay leaves and sugar to it.
2. Place over a gentle heat to cook for a few minutes. Stir as you cook to make the blackberries break down.
3. Allow to cool and set aside.
4. Add cream to it to form soft peaks and fold through natural yogurt.
5. Add cream and serve.

54. Blackcaps Pudding

Ingredients:

- 6 dessert apples
- 2 tbsp. sugar
- 1 tbsp. orange flower water
- Drizzle of Grand Marnier

Preparation:

1. Wash the apples and slice them to prevent them from popping. Sprinkle it with sugar.
2. Place the apples in a baking tray and cover them with orange flower water.
3. Place in the oven and bake at 200°C for 30 minutes.
4. After removing it from the oven, sprinkle with sugar and add the Grand Marnier. Put back in the oven.
5. Leave in the oven for another 30 minutes, after which the apples must look blackened.

55. Sweet Black Cherry Crisp

Ingredients:

- ½ c. granulated sugar
- ½ c. sliced almonds
- ¼ c. softened butter
- ½ c. brown sugar
- 1 c. quick-cooking oats
- 6 c. pitted frozen cherries

Preparation:

1. Add the sugar and three tablespoons of flour into a large bowl.
2. Add cherries to it and mix. Place on a heat source.
3. Add the brown sugar and oats together in a medium bowl and the leftover flour.
4. Add the almonds and sprinkle the cherry mixture.
5. Continue baking until it gets hot, and the top becomes golden brown.

6. Allow standing for about 15 minutes before serving.

56. Warm Blueberry Cobbler

Ingredients:

- 3 c. blueberries
- 6 tbsp. melted butter
- 1 beaten egg
- 1 c. white sugar
- 1 c. all-purpose flour
- 1 tbsp. lemon juice

Preparation:

1. Preheat the oven to 190°C.
2. Transfer the blueberries to a baking dish and sprinkle lemon juice on it.
3. Whisk the egg, sugar, and flour together in a bowl and spread the mixture over the blueberries—spread butter on the flour mixture.
4. Transfer to the preheated oven and leave it there for about 30 minutes.

57. Buffalo Sauce (Buffalo Berry)

Ingredients:

- ½ c. butter
- 1 c. Italian-style salad dressing
- 1 c. red pepper sauce

Preparation:

1. Pour red pepper sauce, butter, and Italian-style salad into a medium saucepan on medium heat.
2. Continue to cool until the butter melts. Allow cooling and serve.

58. Bunchberry and Raspberry Syrup

Ingredients:

- ¼ c. honey
- 4 tbsp. of water
- 2 c. raspberries
- 2 c. bunch of berries

Preparation:

1. Pour all the items into a pan and cook together on the stove for about 10 minutes.
2. Press it through a colander or sieve to help you separate the syrup from the pulp.
3. You can serve it with waffles, pancakes, etc.

59. Chokecherry Syrup

Ingredients:

- Chokecherry
- Sugar
- Lemon juice
- Orange juice
- Pectin

Preparation:

1. Wash the chokecherry thoroughly and add to a saucepan. Cover with water.
2. Boil the chokeberries for about 30 minutes.
3. Strain the juice in it into a separate container and cover it.
4. Add some sugar to it. Next, add lemon juice and orange.
5. Add pectin and mix over medium heat for about 30 minutes.
6. Cool in the refrigerator.
7. Transfer it to a jar and process in boiling water for about 10 minutes.

60. Cloudberry Cake

Ingredients:

- Unsalted butter
- ¾ c. cake flour
- 1 c. granulated sugar
- 6 large eggs
- 1 tsp. baking powder
- Fresh edible flowers
- 1 pt. fresh blackberries
- 1 pt. resin raspberries
- 3 c. cloudberry jam
- 2 tsp. pure vanilla extract
- 4 tbsp. confectionary sugar
- 3 c. heavy cream

Preparation:

1. Preheat the oven to 350°F.
2. Cover the sides of a pan using parchment paper.
3. Brush the pan with butter and sprinkle flowers on it.
4. Add the baking powder and cake flour to a bowl.
5. Add the egg white to a bowl and whisk. Then add salt and granulated sugar.
6. Divide the batter and bake for 20 minutes. Bring it out and let it cool for another 20 minutes.
7. Split the cake horizontally and serve.

61. Cranberry Sauce

Ingredients:

- 1 c. sugar
- 4 c. fresh or frozen cranberries
- 1 c. water
- Pecans, orange zest, currants, raisins, nutmeg, cinnamon, etc. as optional ingredients

Preparation:

1. Rinse the cranberries using clean water and remove any damaged ones among them.
2. Add sugar to the water and boil in a medium saucepan until the sugar dissolves.
3. Add the cranberries to the boiling water and cook until the cranberries burst.
4. Add any of the optional ingredients to dress it.
5. Allow cooling and serve.

62. Crowberry Juice

Ingredients:

- 1 L of raw crowberry juice
- 500g of sugar

Preparation:

1. Pour the raw juice into a pot and add sugar.
2. Allow boiling until the sugar dissolves.
3. Leave it to cool and transfer into sterilized bottles.
4. You can store it for up to 12 months. The shelf life increases as the amount of sugar used increases.

63. Chicken Cutlets with Green Online and Currants Pan Sauce (Currants)

Ingredients:

- 2 tbsp. extra-virgin olive oil
- Kosher salt and fresh ground pepper
- 8 ⅓-inch chicken cutlets
- 1 small, minced shallot
- 1 ½ c. chicken stock
- ¾ c. pitted green picholine olive
- 1 tsp. Dijon mustard
- 2 ½ tbsp. dried currants
- 2 tbsp. drained capers
- 1 tbsp. cold butter

Preparation:

1. Heat the oil in a large skillet and simmer. Add pepper and salt to the chicken cutlets and cook over high heat. Transfer to a plate and place aside.

2. Transfer the shallot to the skillet and cook over medium heat until it is fragrant. Add the stock and continue cooking for another 30 seconds. Add the mustard and simmer for about 3 minutes.

3. Add capers, olives, and currants and simmer for 1 minute. Transfer the chicken to the skillet and simmer for one more minute.

4. Return the chicken to the plate and put off the heat. Add the butter to the sauce and spread the sauce over the chicken cutlets. Serve and enjoy.

64. Dewberries Cobbler (Dewberries)

Ingredients:

- Dewberries
- Sugar
- Butter
- Milk

Preparation:

1. Preheat the oven to 375°F.
2. Add some non-stick spray to a baking pan. Transfer the dewberries to the stockpot and add sugar.
3. Set the heat to medium and allow the sugar and berry to heat up. Stir continuously to avoid sticking to the pan.
4. Turn off the heat and set down the heated mixture.
5. Melt the butter in your microwave for 30 seconds. Pour the melted butter and milk into the ingredient, forming a batter-like dough.
6. Transfer the batter to the pre-sprayed baking pan. Add the dewberries, bake and serve.

65. Elderberry Syrup

Ingredients:

- 2 c. dried organic elderberries
- 3 tsp. organic dried ginger root
- 4 c. cold water
- 1 c. of local honey
- 1 organic sweet cinnamon stick
- 1 c. brandy or vodka

Preparation:

1. Combine the herbs and berries and add cold water to them in a pot. Let it boil.
2. Lower the heat, leaving the herbs to simmer for about 40 minutes.
3. Steep for one hour after removing from heat.
4. Strain the herbs and berries using a funnel covered with an undyed cotton muslin bag and squeeze any leftover liquid. Discard the used herbs.
5. Add honey after cooling the liquid.
6. Add the vodka and stir. Pour into a bottle and store in the refrigerator.

66. Fairy Bell Cocktail

Ingredients:

- Half part apricot brandy
- Ice cubes
- ⅓ part egg white
- 1 ½ part gin
- ⅓ part grenadine

Preparation:

1. Pour the ice cubes into a shaker. Add all the ingredients to it.
2. Shake together and strain into a cocktail glass.

67. Cinnamon Gooseberry Crumbles (Gooseberry)

Ingredients:

- 600 g gooseberries with the stalks removed
- 30 g light brown sugar
- A pinch of mixed spice
- Serve with vanilla ice cream
- 100g of plain flour
- 140 g demerara sugar
- 85 g softened butter
- ½ tsp. ground ginger
- ½ tsp. ground cinnamon
- 1 tsp. baking powder
- 100 g rolled oats

Preparation:

1. Transfer the gooseberries to a pan. Add sugar and mixed spice. Cook for about 8 minutes, and then remove from heat.
2. Put the oats and flour into a mixing bowl and add baking powder, butter, ginger, and cinnamon. Add butter lightly and demerara sugar. Mix well.
3. Transfer the gooseberries into ovenproof ramekins and wrap them in clingfilm. Place them in the freezer. They can be stored for three months.
4. Set the oven's temperature to 180°C and bring it out of the freezer when you want to cook. Remove the cling film and cook for about 50 minutes.
5. Serve with ice cream.

68. Wild Grapes Juice

Ingredients:

- 5 pounds of Wild grapes
- Adequate water

Preparation:

1. Use scissors to harvest the wild grapes to avoid any smashing or bruising.
2. Pour the grapes into a pot and mash until the juice comes out.
3. Add some water to cover the mashed grapes up to an inch.
4. Cover the pot and place it on a burner. Make sure it is only warm. Avoid boiling.
5. Pour the mashed grapes into a large bowl and stem into the colander. Once the juice drains out, remove the mash and allow the juice to cool.
6. Strain the juice through a fine-mesh strainer, pour into containers, and freeze.

69. Groundcherry Cherry Salsa

Ingredients:

- ½ c. red onion
- 1 c. of ground cherries with the outer husk removed
- ⅓ c. roasted tomatoes
- ¼ c. chopped jalapeno without the seeds
- 1 juiced medium lime
- ¼ tsp. sea salt

Preparation:

1. Add all the ingredients together in a food processor to blend.
2. Place in a fridge before serving so that the flavors can combine.
3. You can store it for up to a week.

70. Guelder Rose Jelly

Ingredients:

- 500mls of cold water

- 12 chopped crab apples
- 2 peeled oranges
- 800 g Guelder rose fruits

Preparation:

1. Add the crab apples, oranges, Guelder rose fruits, and water to a pan and simmer for 15 minutes. Mash the mixture occasionally using a potato masher.
2. Strain for about 12 hours by pouring it through a muslin cloth. Avoid squeezing the pulp to prevent making the jelly cloudy.
3. Add 500 g sugar per 500ml of the liquid.
4. Heat the sugar and repeatedly stir until it melts. Leave it to simmer gently for about 20 minutes.
5. Pour the hot Guelder rose liquid into clean jars and allow cooling and storing.

71. Hackberry Jam

Ingredients:

- 1 c. Hackberries
- ½ c. jam
- Water

Preparation:

1. Remove the stems from the berries and wash them. Transfer to a saucepan and add adequate water to cover it.
2. Allow boiling followed by simmering for about 30 minutes.
3. Remove the pump and skin from the seed using a masher.
4. Pour the berries through a strainer into a saucepan to remove the seeds. Try to push some of the pulps through the strainer using a wooden spoon.
5. Add lemon juice to the saucepan and boil. Simmer for about 25 minutes.
6. Pour into a jar and serve with meat, crackers, or biscuit.

72. Hawthorn Berry Ketchup

Ingredients:

- ½ tsp. of salt
- 170 g sugar
- 300 ml of water
- 300 ml of cider vinegar
- 500g of hawthorn berry

- Freshly ground black pepper

Preparation:

1. Remove the berries from the stalks and properly wash them using cold water.
2. Transfer to a large pan and add water and vinegar. Then boil. Let it simmer for about 30 minutes until the berry's skin bursts.
3. Remove from heat and transfer to a sieve to remove the stones and skin.
4. Pour into a pan containing sugar and place it on low heat.
5. After the sugar dissolves, boil and simmer for about 10 minutes.
6. Add salt and pepper to taste. Transfer to sterilized bottles. It can store for up to a year.

73. Huckleberry Cheesecake

Ingredients:

- ½ c. sour cream
- ¼ c. sugar
- 5 eggs
- 2 tsp. vanilla extract
- 4 packages of softened cream cheese
- ¼ c. huckleberries

Preparation:

1. Preheat the oven to 475°F. Place the cheesecake in the middle of the pan and bake.
2. Mix the cinnamon and graham cracker crumbs. Add butter and press the crust to the bottom. Place in the freezer until the filling is ready.
3. Mix vanilla, sour cream, sugar, and cream cheese until they become smooth.
4. Whisk the eggs and pour on the cream. Continue blending until you incorporate the eggs.
5. Add the huckleberries, lemon juice, and sugar together in a saucepan. Place on medium heat and cook until the berries soften.
6. Combine cornstarch and one tablespoon of water and add the cornstarch mixture to the topping.
7. Place on heat to simmer for 2 minutes. Allow cooling at room temperature.

8. Pour one-third of the topping on the cheesecake and create a marbled effect. Pour on transfer to the oven and bake for about 12 minutes. Change the oven temperature to 350°F and bake for 60 minutes.

9. Allow to cool and place in the refrigerator for about 4 hours. Serve and enjoy.

74. Hobblebush Jam

Ingredients:

- Hobbleblush berries
- Sugar
- Pectin

Preparation:

1. Clean the berries and remove the stems. Transfer them to the saucepan.
2. Place on the stove to simmer until the skins pop off.
3. Strain to remove the skins and seeds. Add sugar to the pulp and place it on the stove to boil. Then add pectin and boil for 2 minutes.
4. Remove the foam, pour it into jars, and seal.

75. Mayflower Chicken

Ingredients:

- 2 chicken breasts
- 56 g mayflower Chinese curry powder
- 1 onion
- 50 g peas
- 5 closed cap mushrooms
- 80 g basmati rice
- 200 mills of boiling water
- Low-fat calorie cooking spray

Preparation:

1. Chop the chicken breast into small pieces. Also, chop the onion and mushroom into small pieces

2. Spray a saucepan with cooking spray. Add the chicken and allow it to become brown.

3. Add the vegetables to the saucepan and add 200ml hot water to the mayflower curry. Mix well.

4. Add curry sauce to the pan containing the cooked vegetables and chicken. Allow cooking for about 5 minutes.

5. Drain, and then rinse. Serve and enjoy.

76. Mock Strawberry Jelly

Ingredients:

- 5 c. white sugar
- 5 c. peeled, shredded zucchini
- 3 tbsp. lemon juice
- 2 packages of strawberry flavored Jell-O

Preparation:

1. Transfer the zucchini and sugar to a large pot and stir over medium heat for 10 minutes.

2. Add the gelatin and lemon juice and simmer for about 5 minutes.

3. Transfer into clean jars without filing them to the brim. Close the jar and place it inside boiling water for 10 minutes.

4. Remove from the boiling water, cool, and place in the refrigerator.

77. Mountain Ash or Rowan Berry

Ingredients:

- Fresh rowan berries

Preparation:

1. Wash the rowan berries to get rid of debris. Dry after washing and place in a dehydrator at 150°C for 24 hours.

2. Remove and place inside the fridge in an air-tight container. They can be stored for a couple of months this way.

3. You can use it to make tea, adding warm spices and orange peel.

78. Mulberry Jam

Ingredients:

- 2 pounds of fresh or frozen mulberries
- 6 c. granulated sugar
- ½ c. fresh lemon juice
- 1 pinch of freshly ground nutmeg
- 1 oz. pouch liquid pectin

Preparation:

1. Add the lemon juice, sugar, and mulberries to a large pot.
2. Place on a stove to boil and stir while boiling to dissolve the sugar.
3. Next, add a pinch of the nutmeg. Add the liquid pectin and boil for a minute while you keep on stirring.
4. Remove the foam formed on the surface. Transfer the jam into canning jars without filling the jar to the brim.
5. Secure the jar and process for 5 minutes in boiling water. Cool for 12 to 14 hours.

79. Nannyberry Mousse (Nannyberry)

Ingredients:

- ¾ c. nannyberry butter
- ¼ c. sugar
- 4 tbsp. cornstarch
- 1 tbsp. Fresh lemon juice
- ½ tsp. orange zest to taste
- Pinch of salt
- 4 tbsp. unsalted butter
- 1 c. heavy cream

Preparation:

1. Line a custard dish with soufflé mold.
2. Add the cornstarch, sugar, lemon, orange zest, egg yolk, and water together in a container to make a slurry
3. Heat the nannyberry butter and whisk it until it steams. Do not boil.
4. Stir the slurry and place it on medium heat to thicken. Reduce the heat and continue whisking for a couple of minutes.
5. Remove from the heat source and transfer to a mold. Then place in the refrigerator overnight.

80. Oregon Grape Jelly

Ingredients:

- 5 lbs. of stemmed Oregon grapes
- 3 c. water
- 1 package of liquid pectin
- 5 c. sugar

Preparation:

1. Crush the Oregon grapes and pour some water into them.
2. Pour into a pot and boil for 10 minutes while mashing it slightly.
3. Drain it for a few hours in a colander lined with cheesecloth.
4. Add sugar to the juice obtained and boil rapidly. Add pectin and boil for an additional minute.
5. Transfer to sterilized jars, cover with the lid, and process for 10 minutes in boiling water.
6. Remove from the boiling water and leave it to sit overnight.

81. Traditional Newfoundland Partridgeberry Muffins (Partridgeberry)

Ingredients:

- 1 c. partridgeberries
- 2 c. flour
- 2 c. sugar
- 2 large eggs
- 2 tsp. baking powder
- ½ tsp. sea salt
- 1 tsp. vanilla
- 1 c. butter
- 1 c. evaporated milk

Preparation:

1. Mix the butter and sugar until it is fluffy.

2. Crack the eggs and mix evaporated milk into them.

3. Add into a container the flour, baking powder, and sea salt. Mix and add eggs, milk, sugar, and butter. Mix until fluffy.

4. Add the partridgeberries and flour and toss them together to coat the flour. Fold into your batter.

5. Place inside an oven at 400°F. Allow baking for 25 minutes.

6. Bring out to cool and serve.

82. Passion Fruit and Lemon Condensed Milk Slice (Passion Fruit)

Ingredients:

- 14 digestive biscuits
- 2 395g cans of sweetened condensed milk
- 185 ml of strained fresh lemon juice
- 125 ml of fresh passion fruit pulp

Preparation:

1. Preheat the oven to 160°C. Line a pan with baking paper.

2. Arrange the biscuits on the base of the pan, keeping 2 biscuits aside.

3. Add the lemon juice, condensed milk, and passion fruit juice pump together in a bowl and whisk. Pour the mixture over the biscuits and bake for 15 minutes.

4. Allow to cool at room temperature and put in the fridge overnight.

83. Pawpaw Chutney

Ingredients:

- 2 green pawpaw
- 2 tsp. mustard
- 1 tsp. peppercorns
- 1 c. brown sugar
- ½ c. raisins
- 1 onion
- 1 bottle of vinegar

Preparation:

1. Cut the green pawpaws into discs. Add the mustard, peppercorns, raisins, onion, vinegar, and brown sugar together in a container.
2. Place the mixture on the stove to boil until the pawpaw becomes soft.
3. Allow thickening and cool before transferring to a storage bottle.

84. Steamed Persimmon Pudding (Persimmon)

Ingredients:

- 4 ½ tbsp. unsalted, softened butter
- 2 ¼ tsp. ground cinnamon
- 2 c. all-purpose flour
- ¾ tsp. Ground nutmeg
- ¼ tsp. coarse salt
- ¼ c. calvados brandy
- ¼ c. sultanas
- 4 soft hachiya persimmons
- 1 c. whole milk
- 1 ½ tsp. pure vanilla extract
- 1 tbsp. fresh lemon juice
- 1 ½ tsp. baking soda

- 1 c. toasted, coarsely chopped pecans
- A quarter of finely chopped candied ginger
- Oven-dried persimmon
- Calvados cream

Preparation:

1. Butter a pudding mold with a 12-cup capacity and pour water into a mold to reach halfway.
2. Sift salt, spices, and flour in a bowl and set aside.
3. Place the sultanas and calvados in a small saucepan and simmer. Set aside to cool for 15 minutes.
4. Drain and discard the liquid. Place the raisins aside.
5. Slice away the top of the persimmons and press the flesh through a sieve into a bowl. Throw away the skin, mix it with the milk, and set it aside.
6. Add the sugar and butter together in a bowl and mix until it becomes fluffy and pale. Add lemon juice, vanilla, and egg. Then add the persimmon mixture.
7. Add the baking soda and the flour mixture. Mix everything.
8. Add the ginger, sultanas, and pecans.
9. Pour everything into the mold earlier prepared. Cover with buttered parchment and the lid.
10. Transfer to a wire rack and remove the covering. Allow to cool for 15 minutes and unmold into a plate. Cut it into slices and add the Calvados cream.

85. Pin Cherries Jelly

Ingredients:

- 8 c. sugar
- 5 c. pin cherry juice
- 18 c. pin cherries

Preparation:

1. Wash the cherries and transfer them to a saucepan containing water—Cook for about 30 minutes on low heat.
2. Strain the juice through a jelly bag and let it stay overnight.

3. Transfer the juice produced to a saucepan.

4. Add sugar to it and mix it well. Place on a stove to boil for 15 minutes.

5. Transfer to sterilized jars without filling the jars to the brim.

6. Process in hot water for 10 minutes.

86. Plum and Mascarpone Pie

Ingredients:

- 1 pie crust
- 5 pounds of firm-ripe plums
- 1 ½ c. sugar
- 2 tbsp. fresh lemon juice
- 1 vanilla bean
- 8 oz. mascarpone
- ⅓ c. crème Fraiche
- 2 tbsp. honey
- Whipped cream

Preparation:

1. Preheat the oven to 350°F. Line the pie dish with crust.
2. Place the plums in a large bowl and add one and a half cups of lemon and sugar.
3. Divide the plum mixture into 2 baking dishes and roast for about 60 minutes.
4. Transfer the plum to a baking sheet and transfer the juices to a baking dish. Boil for about 5 minutes.
5. Add the remaining sugar, honey, crème Fraiche and mascarpone to a bowl. Add seeds from vanilla beans and beat at high speed.
6. Spread the mascarpone cream evenly. Spread some glaze over the plums.
7. Cut the pie into slices and spread whipped cream on it. Serve and enjoy.

87. Pricky Pear Cactus

Ingredients:

- 6 cactus pads

- 3 tbsp. olive extra virgin

- Salt, sugar, and pepper to taste

Preparation:

1. Add the sugar, salt, pepper, and oil to a pan.

2. Place the pan on the stove and cook for about 10 minutes.

3. Brush each side of the cactus pads with an oil mixture.

4. Serve and enjoy.

88. Raspberry Pie

Ingredients:

- 200 g chopped unsalted butter

- 400 g dark chocolate

- 30 g top-quality cocoa

- ½ c. sunflower oil

- 1 c. brown sugar

- ½ c. caster sugar

- 1 tsp. vanilla extract

- 3 eggs

- 1 ½ c. plain sifted flour

- 1 c. buttermilk

- ½ tsp. baking powder
- 250 g raspberries

Preparation:

1. Preheat the oven to 160°C. Coat the side of the lamington pan with grease and cover with baking paper.
2. Add oil, chocolate, cocoa, and butter to a bowl and set on a pan to simmer.
3. Add eggs, vanilla, and sugar to another bowl and whisk: mix salt flakes, baking powder, buttermilk, and flour in the melted chocolate. Then fold in half of the raspberries.
4. Spread batter in a pan and place the raspberries on it.
5. Allow baking for 1 hour and 30 minutes.
6. Cool in the pan and place in the fridge for 30 minutes. Slice to serve.

89. Red Blackberries Compote

Ingredients:

- 500 g of vanilla custard
- 180ml of cranberry juice
- 2 tbsp. cornflower
- A dash of rosewater
- ½ tbsp. Golden caster sugar
- ½ tsp. Ground cinnamon
- ½ tbsp. vanilla extract

Preparation:

1. Cook the fruit over medium heat in a large saucepan. Pour 150ml of cranberry juice, rosewater, sugar, cinnamon, and vanilla extract and cook for 20 minutes,
2. Add the cornflower to the remaining cranberry juice. Pour on the hot fruit and stir until it mixes well. Turn off the heat and allow cooling. Transfer it to a bowl and cover it. Place in the fridge for some hours before serving.

90. Rose Hips

Ingredients:

- Rosehips
- Water

Preparation:

1. Pour water over the rose hips.
2. Allow the rose hips to steep for 15 minutes. Cover and strain the pulp.

91. Salal

Ingredients:

- 12 c. cleaned salal berries
- ¾ tsp. fresh lemon juice
- 4 tbsp. sugar to taste

Preparation:

1. Cook the berries over medium-high heat. Strain it through a cheesecloth and extract the juice.
2. Transfer the berries to a saucepan on medium heat. Add sugar and lemon juice to taste and cook to dissolve the sugar for 5 minutes.
3. Sterilize half-pint jars for 10 minutes. Pour the hot jam into it without reaching the brim.
4. Place in boiling water and process for 5 minutes. Store in the fridge.

92. Salmonberry

Ingredients:

- ½ c. white sugar
- 4 c. divided salmonberries
- 1 package of white cake mix
- ¾ c. water
- 2 tbsp. vegetable oil
- 3 eggs

Preparation:

1. Preheat an oven to 350°F and grease the cake pans.

2. Press the salmonberries through a strainer and discard the leftover in the strainer.

3. Transfer the juice and the pulp from the bowl into a measuring cup. Pour water into it and stir.

4. Add the salmonberry mixture, vegetable oil, eggs, and cake mix to a bowl. Blend for about 30 seconds.

5. Bear the cake mixture for 2 minutes. Fold the whole salmonberries into a cake mixture and evenly pour into the prepared pans.

6. Bake in the oven for about 30 minutes.

7. Cook the salmonberry mixture and sugar over medium-high heat in a saucepan. Remove from the heat.

8. Pour the cooled salmonberry mixture onto the cake layer. Allow cooling completely.

93. Saskatoons

Ingredients:

- 24 oz. of fresh Saskatoon berries
- 1 tbsp. lemon juice
- ¼ c. maple syrup
- 2 tbsp. flour

Preparation:

1. Preheat the oven to 350°F and grease a baking pan lightly.

2. Add maple syrup, flour, lemon juice, and Saskatoon berries into a medium-size mixing bowl.

3. Add the mixture to the greased baking pan to bake for 60 minutes.

4. Add crème fraiche to serve.

94. Sea Buckthorn Juice

Ingredients:

- Berries
- Sweetener

- Water

Preparation:

1. Wash the berries and blend them.

2. Add sweetener and blend for 1 minute.

3. Strain the juice and set the pulp aside.

4. Add water to the juice and serve chilled.

95. Basic Solomon's Seal Shoots

Ingredients:

- Kosher salt to taste

- 4 oz. of Solomon's plume

- Freshly squeezed lemon juice

- Butter or extra virgin olive oil

Preparation:

1. Prepare a pot and bring it to a boil.

2. Cook the shoots for a couple of minutes.

3. Add lemon juice, salt, butter, or oil to season.

96. Strawberry Mint Gin

Ingredients:

- ½ c. crushed ice

- ¼ c. Tanqueray gin

- 3 tsp. agave nectar

- 1 tbsp. fresh lemon juice

- 8 large mint leaves

- 6 fresh strawberries

Preparation:

1. Blend the ice and put in the strawberries, honey, nectar, lemon juice, and mint to form a paste.

2. Add the Tanqueray gin.

3. Add half a cup of crushed ice and pack it into a glass.

97. Teaberry Ice Cream

Ingredients:

- 1 ½ c. whole milk
- 4 large egg yolk
- 1 ½ c. heavy cream
- 3 drops of red food coloring
- ½ tsp. vanilla extract
- 1 tsp. teaberry extract
- ⅔ c. granulated sugar
- Pinch of salt

Preparation:

1. Transfer ice cubes to a bowl and fill with cold water.
2. Heat the cream and milk in a saucepan on low heat.
3. Whisk the sugar and egg yolk in a large bowl and remove from heat. Add the extracts.
4. Steam the warmed milk mixture into the egg yolk and whisk.
5. Pour the tempered yolk into the saucepan and let it cook at 170°F.
6. Pour into a strainer and put the strained liquid in a bowl of ice water. Chill in the refrigerator for several hours after it cools.
7. Pour the custard into the ice cream maker and process in hot water.

98. Thimbleberry Jam

Ingredients:

- Thimbleberries
- sugar

Preparation:

1. Clean the berries properly and sterilize the lids and jars.

2. Add equal portions of the berries and sugar.

3. Transfer the jam into the sterilized jars and place it in a water bath. Leave it to process for about 10 minutes.

4. Remove and cool.

99. Wineberry

Ingredients:

- 2 c. wineberries
- 4 tbsp. cold water
- 1 egg
- ¼ c. butter
- Pinch of salt
- 2 tbsp. sugar
- 2 c. flour

Preparation:

1. Pulse the salt, sugar, and flour in a food processor.
2. Add the butter and egg, then add water.
3. Divide the batter in half and place it in the fridge for about 1 hour.
4. Place all the ingredients in a bowl and coat the berries with cornstarch and honey.
5. Preheat the oven to 350°F.
6. Bake for about 30 minutes.

100. Hickory Nuts Pie

Ingredients:

- 3 lightly beaten eggs
- ¾ c. sugar
- 1 unbaked pie shell
- 2 tbsp. softened butter
- 1 c. chopped hickory nut meats
- 1 tsp. vanilla

- 1 c. white syrup

Preparation:

1. Preheat the oven to 400°F.
2. Mix the butter, vanilla, sugar, syrup, and egg, and add nutmeat. Add filling to a pie shell.
3. Allow baking for 10 minutes. Lower the heat to 350°F for 40 minutes.
4. Cool, slice, and serve.

101. Candied Hazelnut

Ingredients:

- ½ c. packed brown sugar
- ½ tsp. salt
- 1 large beaten egg white
- ½ tsp. vanilla extract
- ¼ tsp. ground cinnamon
- 12 oz. blanched hazelnuts

Preparation:

1. Preheat the oven to 250°F.
2. Whisk the cinnamon, vanilla, salt, egg white, and brown sugar.
3. Add the nuts and spread the nut mixture on parchment paper.
4. Place in the oven to bake at 250°F for about 50 minutes.
5. Cool after removing from the oven. You can store it for up to 1 week.

102. Chestnut and Maple Butter

Ingredients:

- 400 g. of peeled and cooked chestnuts
- ½ c. mild-flavored olive oil
- ½ c. water
- ½ tsp. salt
- 1 tbsp. maple syrup

Preparation:

1. Preheat the oven to 200°C.
2. Place the prepared chestnut on a baking tray and bake for about 20 minutes.
3. After cooking, let the chestnuts cool and wrap in a clean towel for 5 minutes.
4. Peel off the chestnut's outer brown shell and remove the thin papery skin under it.
5. Place peeled chestnuts into a food processor and chop them. Add water, salt, and oil.
6. Process until creamy and smooth. Add water and transfer to a clean air-tight jar.
7. Store for 2 weeks.

103. Butternut Squash Soup

Ingredients:

- 2 to 3 pounds of butternut squash
- Nutmeg
- 6 c. chicken stock
- 1 medium chopped onion
- 2 tbsp. unsalted butter

Preparation:

1. Cut the squash into chunks.
2. Melt butter in a large pot. Add the onions and cook for about 8 hours.
3. Add squash and stock. Simmer and cook for 20 minutes until tender.
4. Remove squash chunks using a slotted spoon.
5. Place in a blender and puree.
6. Return the blended squash to the pot.
7. Stir and add pepper, salt, and nutmeg to season.

104. Black Walnut

Ingredients:

- 1 c. shredded cheddar cheese
- 2 packages of cream cheese at room temperature
- ½ tsp. Worcestershire sauce
- ¼ c. green diced peppers
- ¼ c. diced pimento
- 1 tbsp. diced onion
- ¼ tsp. garlic salt
- 1 c. chopped black walnuts

Preparation:

1. Add all the ingredients and mix thoroughly.

2. Roll into a ball and cool until it becomes firm.

3. Roll the cheese ball in chopped black walnuts.

4. Press the nuts into the surface.

5. Chill and then serve.

105. Beechnuts Butter

Ingredients:

- Beech nuts
- Sugar or honey
- Oil

Preparation:

1. Gather and shell the nuts. Roast for 15 minutes.

2. Rub on the skin.

3. Put it in the blender until the nuts turn to a paste.

4. Add some oil and add honey or sugar.

5. Add the nuts and transfer them to the jars. Store in a refrigerator.

Chapter 7: Two-Week Edible Wild Plant Meal Plan

Note:

- This meal plan gives some ideas about how you can consume the recipes in this book, but it is not meant to be a total list of the foods you will eat. You should supplement your edible wild plant foods and drinks with other "normal" foods.
- Living on only edible wild plants is possible but may be difficult unless you have access to many edible wild foods.

Day	Breakfast	Lunch	Dinner	Total Calories (Kcal)
1	Chickichurri	Caramelized Chicory With Orange And Thyme	Mayflower Chicken Garlic Mustard Pesto	403.5
2	Comfrey Plantain Salve	Claytonia And Arugula Salad	Cleaver Juice	485

3	Wild Lettuce Tea	White Clover Pudding	Wild Curly Dock Masala	371
4	Herb Robert Tea	Henbit Salad	Dandelion Greens	557
5	Horsetail Tea	Deep-Fried Kudzu Tofu	Japanese Knotweed	264
6	Creamy Lambs Quarter Gratin	Lady's Thumb Salad	Andalusian Mallow With Chickpea	387
7	Mullein Tea	Melilot Blancmange	Mugwort Soup	542
8	Pineapple Weed Tea	Pigweed Smoothie	Chilled Lemony Wood Sorrel Soup	442
9	Plantain Tea	Quick Weed Potato Salad	Chicken Cutlets with Green Olives and Currants Pan Sauce	477
10	Valerian Tea	Garlicky Nettles Pesto	Creamy Lambs Quarter Gratin	295
11	Wild Bergamot Tea	Chilled Lemony Wood Sorrel Soup	Sauteed Watercress With Garlic	403
12	Wild Lettuce Tea	Arctic Raspberry	Sweet And Sour Crabapple	748.6
13	Pineapple Weed Tea	Aronia Berries Smoothie	Pork Chops With Barberry	663
14	Yarrow Tea	Sweet Black Cherry Crisp	Mini Blackberry & Bay Pavlova	725

Made in the USA
Middletown, DE
07 January 2024

47411857R00064